The Tc

Vicky Kaseorg

To Tom —
Pleasure meeting you and I pray
this book is an inspiration
to you! Regards
Vicky Kaseorg

VICKY KASEORG

There is a time for everything,
and a season for every activity under heaven:
a time to be born and a time to die,
a time to plant and a time to uproot,
a time to kill and a time to heal,
a time to tear down and a time to build,
Ecclesiastes 3: 1-3

Dedication

There are many people who were instrumental in the writing and research for this book. I have mentioned many of them in the story itself, but there are two that I could not have even conceived of the idea had I not had their input, support, and continual guidance.

The first is my brother John Ceccherelli, who sent me on a wild "field trip to take pictures and get the scoop on the mystery of some famous towers" with more faith in my ability than I had in myself. His encouragement that I would understand the beauty, wonder, and mystique of radio towers of which I was completely ignorant was an enormous leap of blind faith. I love you, John!

The second person who deserves special recognition is the tower builder himself, Tony Fonseca. Tony could not have been more patient and kind, never complaining about having to deal with such a bumbling neophyte in the tower world as I was. Despite a killer work schedule and overfull life, he always made time for me and my constant pestering with questions and interview sessions. I was amazed at what Tony accomplished before I ever met him. Over the years that I grew to know him, I counted him a cherished friend. I grew to respect him, if possible, even more than my glowing initial impressions. You are a good man, Tony. Thank you. Inexpressible gratitude.

Table of Contents

*Some names have been changed to protect the privacy of the characters. If there are any inaccuracies, it is the fault of the author alone. However, I strived to present the events as truthfully as the limitations of my understanding permitted.

Why You Really *Do* Want to Read a Book About Towers

Eight years prior to writing this book, my brother John, a radio engineer, asked me to take photographs and arrange a tour of some rare radio towers near my home in Charlotte. I knew nothing about radio towers, and had been content in my ignorance. But I loved my brother and so I went. I am not certain why I was instantly captivated...perhaps overexposure to radiation at the tower site. As a result, I will never look at radio towers the same way again, especially not the beautiful and iconic WBT-AM three tower array.

I am certain you will feel similarly when you read this story. Who would have thought towers could teach so much about life, love, and faith?

Radio/tower/engineering geeks would certainly enjoy this book, but it is also meant for average folks with no knowledge of any of those fields. I, the author, am one of those average folk. Maybe even below average. I began this journey with *zip, zero, nada* understanding of towers or their builders. I had no idea that I would find them compelling.

While recounting a remarkable engineering feat, this book also chronicles my journey learning about a subject of which I had been completely ignorant. In the process, I discovered tantalizing and obscure tales from the past while solving a seventy-year-old mystery. It is a story of remarkable human beings, dangerous livelihoods, the creative spirit, relationships, courage, passion, and faith. Towers are the setting, but the message is universal, one that even those of us who are afraid of heights can relate to without having to climb one inch up those frightening antennas. Believe me, if climbing them had been required of the author, this book would not have been written.

The WBT-AM Blaw Knox Towers - Photo by Vicky Kaseorg

CHAPTER ONE
A Towering Builder

"Oh crap!" said the tower builder who was at this moment free falling from the top of a 1,000-foot radio tower. Tony had never intended to die this way, and was pretty ticked off with the hoist operator responsible for this hurtling to certain death.

It had started off as an ordinary day. Hot, humid – typical Florida summer. The morning had proceeded routinely. The job was to inspect the top portion of the tower, specifically the antenna input. Willie, the foreman, was working alongside Tony, both dangling 1,000 feet in the air at the top of the thin spire. The other tower riggers -- Vinnie, Joey, and Junior -- were all near the top of the imposing tower. None seemed concerned that cars far below them were the size of tiny toys, and people like ants. None seemed fazed by the fact that a thin one inch strap and lanyard were all that held them a thousand feet above the hard, unforgiving ground. All were concentrating on their work when Willie pointed into the distance.

"Oh boy, look at what's headed our way!" he called to Tony.

Tony shielded his eyes against the sun and looked out over the horizon. Florida landscape lent itself to incredible vistas from such a high vantage point – huge flat expanses of land allowing unobstructed views to the horizon. The view right now was of a massive bank of black clouds with rain tumbling off of it in a solid sheet. The distant lightning was beautiful against the dark backdrop, but not something any tower builder ever wants to see when at the top of a tower.

"Better get down fast," said Tony, "That's rolling in pretty quickly." He knew from experience that Florida storms could rocket in within minutes out of nowhere. Willie radioed the hoist operator, "Storm racing this way, Louie. You need to get us down in a hurry."

"Will do," said Louie, "Hang on."

The five men all hooked on to the load line. This was in the early 1980s when the hoist was a "friction hoist," not nearly as safe or controlled as modern hoists. The tower workers were dependent on the operator keeping the right amount of pressure on the brake pedal, but even then the descent was not as controlled as modern equipment allows. The hoist operator would slowly (hopefully) lower the cable, or load line, with the riggers clamped on.

"All aboard?" Louie asked.

"Get going," ordered Willie, watching the lightning strikes snaking nearer like Medusa's hair from the ominous cloud.

That was the last thing Tony heard before a sickening lurch and then he was cascading hundreds of feet while the tower whizzed by him in a blur. He didn't have time to think or wonder why he was free-falling. He did have time to formulate the concept that life was over for him, and he was not at all pleased.

Willie was yelling frantically, "Brake! Brake!" but for many seconds, the men catapulted 100, 200, 300 feet...and still they were falling! With the ground approaching at a most dismaying speed, and one hundred feet left before they would all be flattened on the earth, the operator managed to brake at last. The impact of suddenly stopping such a precipitous descent caused them all to spring back up several feet that felt like fifty, before finally dangling to a stop. None of them could speak. None were yet quite sure how they were still alive. Slowly, they were lowered the final sixty feet to the ground.

There was ominous silence as their feet touched the grass at the base of the tower.

"I told you to hurry up...not kill us!" Willie suddenly erupted, unsnapping his safety line from the load line. While the other four men leaned over catching their breath, Willie stormed over to Louie. Tony could not hear what was said, but he could surmise from the tone of voice, the pumping fists, and the exaggerated swings of Willie's arms, that Louie may not be on the job much longer.

Tony stood up, and cracked a weak smile at his co-workers, "Now *that* was exciting, don't you think?"

*****

Fortunately, that was not the first time he had stepped onto a tower, though he was still a young engineer at the time. He recalls his first tower climb with a little more relaxed heart rate...

On that first climb, Tony pulled on his gloves and snapped the buckle of his hard hat, looking straight up but unable to see the top of the tower. The antenna stretched high above him, 1,000 feet into the clouds. Perched on a mountain top with an already impressive view stretching below, the view from the tower apex had to be nothing short of magnificent! It was an impressive first tower to climb, but Tony had fortunately never been afraid of heights. Still, he swallowed several times as he snapped on the safety harness.

What could go wrong?

Well, for starters, on an AM broadcast tower, if he missed hopping on to the first cross piece and the teensiest bit of his flesh touched the ground and tower simultaneously, he would be rewarded with a strong jolt of electricity that might not *quite* melt his hair, but could uncurl it as the current grounded. Unlike some of the other problems a tower climber might encounter, electrocution was *not* the most frightening one on the list.

If he successfully got past that crucial first step, his survival was still not assured. He stood a greater chance of greeting another day if without fail, he religiously 'tied on' with the safety hooks. Should he lose focus and forget to clasp the safety hook, one misstep could mean a plummet from hundreds of feet in the air, with only the clouds to catch him. Well, he *could* get lucky and grab at the frame whizzing by. If his arm remained attached to his body, he could be looking at only permanent disability, as opposed to tragic loss of life.

Exactly how fast *would* he be going as he plummeted to earth? It depends, he vaguely recalled from his physics class.

The speed he would fall depended on two things: how fast he was going when he started falling and how long he would continue to fall. He did a quick calculation: over 120 mph within seconds. Of course, air resistance played a part in the equation, but for now, he felt it was safe to assume that if he was at the top of the tower when the free-fall commenced, he would need to be scraped off the ground with a putty knife.

And that's if he made it to the ground with no obstructions along the way. It was possible he would bounce off one of the metal braces, while careening down at over one hundred miles an hour. He had strong bones, being a fit man, but probably not strong enough to ever play tennis again after such a tumble.

Of course, there were circumstances he could *not* control that might additionally contribute to his death or maiming. If the tag line that held equipment being raised up the tower didn't maintain the correct tension, the load could slam against the struts and diagonals, and down, down, down the tower might go. And predictably, if the tower went down...so would the tower climber. Different formulas probably applied when falling while clinging to the side of a several ton tower, though as Tony recalled, the speed of collapse was not greatly affected by weight.

He glanced up again and noticed a hawk, a mere dot in the sky circling around one edge of the tower. A frenzied flock of smaller birds zipped by, above the hawk. The top was higher than even the birds.

Tony calculated the width of the metal cross beams on the intricate lattice beside him. Only 2 1/2 inches wide. His shoe would overlap the edge as he clambered across the struts at a height stretching nearly seven football fields above the ground. Tony took a deep breath and checked all the buckles again on the harness.

"Nervous?" asked the project manager coming alongside the young engineer.

"Not too bad," said Tony.

"Just stay focused," said the manager, "And stay tied on. You know the drill -- tie on or die."

"Thanks for the reminder," laughed Tony.

They both looked up when the hawk screeched above them.

"He might play a little kamikaze game with you," said the manager, "They can be pesky."

Tony watched the hawk, and imagined the sharp curved beak and nasty talons swiping at his hands while he dangled 1,000 feet in the air. His instructors had not mentioned the danger of hawks gouging soft body parts.

"Does your wife know you are going to be up there?" asked the manager, watching the rest of the crew preparing the tag line, the cable, and the equipment they would need in inspecting the tower.

"I'm not married," said Tony.

"No? A handsome young guy like you? Why not?"

"Haven't found *the one* yet," said Tony.

"The one? I found four of them. Working on number five but she might really be *the one*," said the manager. Tony laughed, and appreciated the banter. He knew what the manager was doing. New engineer, first tower climb, first job out of college. Anyone would be nervous, and even Tony, not prone to nerves, was not completely at ease, at least not as much as *before* he

16

had calculated the speed of free-fall or learned about the kamikaze hawks. He looked up again.

"Ready to go?" asked Skosh, the chief engineer who was accompanying Tony for his first climb. Fog was now rolling in and the top of the tower was obscured. They would ascend in an elevator to get to the top.

"Ready," said Tony, "Can't wait!"

Skosh opened the accordion doors of the elevator and the two men stepped on the platform. The grate beneath and around them allowed Tony to look out over the impressive view as they ascended 100 feet per minute. He was alert, paying attention, and maybe a little overawed, but not exactly fearful. While heights had never frightened him, he had not ever been this high, or on such a thin structure. When they reached the top, Skosh pulled open the screeching door.

He hooked his safety belt to the ladder outside the elevator and nodded to Tony to do the same. Tony's knuckles were white as he gripped the ladder for the first time. The fog was clearing again, and the mountains around him were slowly materializing like ghosts out of the whiteness. He stepped onto the 2 ½ inch angle brace, and looked down. He recalled one tower rigger's advice – *only look down at your shoes, no further. No one is afraid of the height from his eyes to his shoes.*

Too late. Down was quite a ways down! For those first ten minutes, Tony did not relax his grip on the ladder, but then, gazing out at the mountains greeting him one by one as they emerged from the fog, he was no longer anxious. All he felt was wonder and inexpressible awe. The purplish-blue mountains stretched out all around him, and he noticed a river in the distance, silvery and glinting in the sun.

By now, he was looking down with glee, noticing people were just dots below him. If only his father could see him up here!

He looked down, thinking again how far down *down* was! A hawk swooped right by him, the whoosh of wings sending a current of air raising the hair on his arms.

"Hey, scram!" yelled Tony, as surprised as the hawk that he was able to speak.

"Ok, not so bad?" asked Skosh.

"It is fantastic," said Tony.

They set to work, inspecting the metal structure and bolted connections for signs of wear, or corrosion. The hawk thankfully disappeared over the mountain. The clouds drifted beneath him. The hum of the hoist engine was lost in the wind that slithered across the tip of the tower as Tony clung to it, his mouth agape, his eyes filled with wonder, certain he could see the curve of the earth in the hazy blue distance.

No longer feeling anything but exultation, Tony laughed and cried out, "Awesome! This is so awesome!"

*****

The ten-year-old boy sat in the back seat, his four siblings all reciting the rosary out loud. They had been traveling for hours, on a journey from upstate New York to Florida. It was a trip they took as a family frequently, and surprisingly, the rosary recitation helped the endless hours pass. They all recited in Spanish.

Creo en Dios, Padre todopoderoso, creador del Cielo y de la tierra...

Occasionally, the mom would change it up and pray the rosary in French, as she had learned decades ago when still a little girl. The father, always eager to guide and nurture and instruct these children he was preparing for greatness, jumped into the pause as the group considered what language to switch to now. Religion, the mother could nurture and dispense; the father would engineer vision and excellence.

"What do you want to be one day, Tony?" he asked the ten-year-old. The father, an immigrant and successful business owner in his adopted country, had great hopes for this son. The boy eagerly followed him like a puppy on the construction site, carefully absorbing every lesson that the patient civil engineer tried to teach him. It is true little Tony had to work hours after school, struggling to remember what came so quickly, so naturally to his brother and sisters. How many hours had he spent reading passages from the National Geographic, while his father sat with him? And when he had finished struggling with the reading, his father would have him write the passage carefully to improve his handwriting skills. (To this day, Tony receives unsolicited compliments on his handwriting which he attributes to his father's patient care and work with him.) Tony never balked. He knew what he was expected to do and he quietly did so, but it was not easy.

Still, he did not complain. He remembered his father often telling the children, "The best legacy you can leave your children is an education."

His father was always beside him through those endless homework hours, despite his own long days working. The other children didn't need his help as much, but Tony did. The father loved Tony, though the spoon smacked down on his small hand when he read a word incorrectly might not have felt like love at just that moment.

Other boys might have resented the talented siblings who collected A's effortlessly like freckles. Other boys might have bemoaned the extra hours they had to spend beside the irrepressible father, intent that Tony would be excellent. But not Tony. He didn't complain and he didn't avoid the work. He would not disappoint the father he loved. Yes, Daddy was strict, but Daddy was also good, and respected; an honest man who loved his children and wanted the world for them. All things were possible in America, and his children would make something grand of themselves.

After listening to his father's question, Tony leaned forward. His eager face was framed in tight dark curls.

"When you grow up," his father repeated, "what do you dream of being?"

"I just want to be a plain man," Tony said quietly.

His father's face grew red and without thinking, he blindly swung his arm and swatted the boy on the back of his head.

"I want to be a doctor!" called out one sister. The others quickly chimed in with illustrious careers, and the father calmed. He glanced in the mirror at his remarkable brood, destined for greatness. But how to help Tony....?

One day, those five would be gathered with the mother, the father long gone, childhood behind them all. One became a dentist, another an architect, another a physical therapist, and the baby became a mechanical engineer.

Tony, the boy who had thought he would one day like to be a "plain man" became one of the nation's leading tower engineers. He would design the towers that he would then climb and dangle from, thousands of feet above the earth, oblivious to the fear and the danger. He didn't know his work was considered the most dangerous job in America nor did he care. He *was*, at heart, a plain man, an honest man, and an attentive man. He would maintain his focus, unaware and uncaring that he was a plain man becoming a great man.

His optimism pierced through the hurricane that trampled the towers he would almost impossibly rebuild, through the stormy marriage that ended in irrevocable broken hearts, and through the dissolution of all he had known and loved. He would rebuild without blueprints, not only the historic towers that no one else would dare attempt, but his shattered heart as well. He didn't spend much time crying when his life dissolved around him, though he did spend a good bit of time rejoicing when love tiptoed through doors he thought were closed, and tapped him gently on his unsuspecting shoulder. And he would *build, build, build* up to the heavens, stretching so much higher than even his father had ever dreamt he might reach.

CHAPTER TWO
A Towering Storm
September 1989

The rare towers were days away from being ripped apart by the tumultuous hurricane, but no one knew it yet. The young engineer who would be asked to rebuild them was contemplating marriage, with no foreshadowing of the storm that would blow that love so ferociously away. An ancient beacon from an era long gone remained unperturbed, its presence constant, but its origin shrouded in mystery. The story of all three would collide unexpectedly in the aftermath of the storm, but no one knew it yet.

Just off Cape Verde Island, a baby that would become a monster was born. A tropical "wave" -- area of low pressure -- was forming. Across the wide ocean, on a distant continent, the three historic radio towers were broadcasting as though their future were not in jeopardy. They had stood for fifty years, and the clear sunny day gave no indication they might not stand for fifty more. No one watching the inauspicious origin of the wave would have prophesied that two weeks later, the storm spawned from it would produce billions of dollars in damage, destroy the entire infrastructure of several islands, and leave hundreds of thousands homeless, not to mention eradicating a whole species of creatures. The barometric pressure slowly dropped, and within a few days the wave moving off the west coast of Africa became a tropical depression. By September 11, storm watchers determined the wave had intensified to a Tropical Storm, with winds now over 30 mph, and the baby wave was now mature enough to be named. Hugo was, unfortunately, not done growing.

Thousands of miles away, rare bats were gathering in their Guadalupe and Montserrat trees and fields, folding their wings and closing their enormous eyes. The species, the Guadeloupe Big-Eyed Bat (*Chiroderma Improvisum*) was found nowhere else in the world. They did not yet feel Hugo's wind rustling the leaves of the secure limbs they hung from in the peaceful islands of the Lesser Antilles.

Banana farmers in Puerto Rico were just finishing planting their fields. The bananas were planted year round in irrigated sections, but on the non-irrigated mountain fields, August to September were ideal planting months. Mature bananas could be harvested year round. Some had heard reports of a storm gathering, but it was still days away and they had all weathered many hurricanes.

In St. Thomas, WBNB-TV was watching the projected path of the storm and reporting to its viewers that Hugo had accelerated, and by Sept. 13 was a Category 2 hurricane. By September 15th, its winds surpassed 157 mph, and Hugo was classified as CAT 5. WBNB-TV warned the community that as of now, Hugo was projected to pass directly over St. Thomas.

All along the coast of South Carolina and Georgia, warnings were issued for residents to evacuate. Do not fool around with this one! Hugo's path could hit anywhere along the southeast coast, with Charleston smack dab in the middle of most projections. The forecasters predicted the storm would be a massive CAT 4 hurricane, with devastating damage, ten-foot or higher storm surges, and widespread destruction. The residents of the coastal cities retreated in droves to inland cities. The hotels in Charlotte, North Carolina bulged with people seeking shelter from the storm.

WBT-AM-Radio, Charlotte, the powerhouse AM radio station of the South, posted numerous updates on the storm. Safely inland, Charlotte listeners prayed for the islands and coastal communities of the Lesser Antilles, Central America, and their southeast coastal friends.

When Hugo slammed into Guadalupe on September 17th, the storm surge was eight feet high. Thirty percent of the buildings and 10,000 homes were pulverized. Debris blocked thirty percent of the roads. The airport control tower was knocked completely out of commission.

When the gale hit Montserrat, nearly ninety percent of the structures on the island were obliterated. The Big-Eyed Bat population was decimated. Most reports later indicated that on Montserrat, the rare bat was feared extinct. It was highly likely that those big eyes got bigger during the pummeling winds, and had the species survived, may well have been renamed 'the *Wild*-Eyed bat.'

On St.Thomas Island, next stop on the fearsome route of the massive spinning wall of wind, the WBNB-TV transmitter was toppled, twisted beyond repair. WBNB-TV went off the air, never again to reopen.

In Puerto Rico, the banana farmers watched helplessly as nearly the entire banana crop was wiped out. Bananas swirled through the air like fragrant missiles. The coffee crop fared no better, making the following morning even more awful to awaken to.

On September 22, When Hugo landed in the United States at Isle of Palms in the Charleston Harbor area, it was a CAT 4 hurricane. The storm surge was 12-14 feet high. 3,000 tornadoes were reported to be imbedded in the storm, causing damage over widespread areas all around the hurricane eye. Boats were wrenched from their moorings and tossed like twigs in splintered piles hundreds of feet from their berths. Then Hugo turned northward, and was churning on a direct path to Charlotte.

WBT-AM Charlotte's three historic towers continued to broadcast warnings. The storm was weakening, but at this point, was headed to Charlotte and might still be hurricane force when it hit. Some residents nervously stockpiled batteries, bread, and milk, but hurricanes *never* hit Charlotte and many did not take the warnings seriously. Six hours after Hugo hit Charleston, it blasted into Charlotte.

WBT-AM chief engineer, Bob White, was carefully monitoring the radio transmissions. The signal was fading in and out as the CAT 1 hurricane battered the transmitters. There were power outages throughout the city as the storm unleashed its fearsome winds and rain, and tossed tornadoes off of it like confetti. Bob was in the downtown studio to trouble shoot during the power outages and try to keep the station operative. He called his engineer, Ted Bryan, and asked that Ted head out to the FM transmitter. He himself would drive to the AM transmitters, the historic and iconic array of three rare diamond shaped towers.

At that point, the hurricane winds were growing and there was trouble on the AM audio transmission. It was early morning, dark, and treacherous. Stop lights flickered and bobbed in the tumult outside, some blinking off and remaining extinguished. Bob hopped into his truck and headed to South Charlotte, where the array of three transmitting towers shuddered in the wrath of the storm.

Meanwhile, Ted, on route to the FM transmitter site, crossed a bridge that was drenched in the creek overflow of hurricane swollen water. The car was washed off the bridge and into the creek. Somehow, Ted managed to get out of the car and walked the final mile to the transmitter. He could not quite remember how he had wrenched open the door in the rising water.

As Bob drove, a large tree, complete with root ball, flew across the road in front of him. "This might not be good," he thought. By the time he arrived at the towers, near horizontal rain was pelting him with what seemed like personal animosity. The sky was inky black and the wind roared and snapped at his coat as he opened the gate to the field. A plastic grocery bag splatted against his ankles, clutched desperately for a moment, and then flew away, vanishing in the grip of the terrible wind.

He drove across the field, while the wind periodically lifted the side of his truck, where it would totter on two wheels. The noise of the wind was so thunderous that all other sound was obliterated. Forcing the door open into the wind, he could barely stand when he stood unprotected in the storm. He shut down the transmission to Tower A, then pulled his raincoat around him and surveyed his towers. The microwave dish on Tower B was blown out of place which explained the fading signal that had been reported.

It was now 4:30 a.m. Bob knew he needed to go inside the transmitter building on the edge of the field and attempt to get the audio signal off the telephone instead. He hopped desperately back in his Blazer, and began driving from Tower B, past Tower A, towards the building. The wind was howling, the rain pelting the windshield like bullets. The hurricane was shaking his car like a rattle as the winds buffeted its sides. Even above the shriek of the wind, Bob heard a cadence of pings as small airborne projectiles spattered against his car. A large object moving in the periphery of his vision caught his attention. Bob glanced in his rear view mirror. With a sickening lurch, he saw the entire top section of the 430-foot Tower A filling his mirror as it came crashing down. Bob gunned the Blazer and missed being crushed by thousands of pounds of steel by approximately two seconds. The impact was so strong and the steel base so unwilling to lose its grasp on the toppled section that the entire top half was pulled back across the grass, then settled with a shudder in the trench it had dug across the field.

Shaking uncontrollably, Bob pulled up to the transmitter building, and again wrestled with the wind to open the door. By now, the wind was so powerful that he could not stand. He crawled across the rain battered ground and up the steps on his hands and knees. Gratefully, he lurched into the building. Still overcome by how narrowly he had escaped death, his fingers would not cease their spasmodic shaking and he was unable to push the release buttons to get to the wires behind the telephone. He ripped the telephone box off the wall, thinking he could repair it later. For now he needed to reach the wires and transfer audio to the telephone line.

Bob managed to regain audio. He called Ted Bryan, who had by now reached the fortunately undamaged FM transmitter.

"Tower A came down!" Bob sputtered, "Nearly killed me!"

There was a brief pause, and then Ted replied, "Ten four."

Typical understated Ted, thought Bob as he got off the phone.

There would be little sleep that night. WBT-AM radio incredibly remained on the air throughout the hurricane's horrific onslaught.

The sky slowly brightened as the hurricane passed. Bob White stepped out onto the loading dock as the first light of the day illuminated the field. He glanced at Tower A, the first and oldest tower in his array. Of course, having barely escaped its guillotined head as the giant storm sliced it, he already knew it was down. Still, it seared his heart to look at it. Built in 1934, it was one of the oldest standing towers in the United States. It had been with the station for over half a century. How could they have lost their rare, precious tower!? He pushed the door further open and glanced at Tower B, the second in the array. It still stood, with the microwave dish slightly off kilter but otherwise apparently unscathed. It was transmitting bravely on its own, as it had all night.

The devastation of Charleston had been so overwhelming that not a single radio station in the path of the storm for hundreds of miles except WBT-AM remained on the air. Information from residents in need had been relayed to WBT-AM, who then transmitted the information to the stores and facilities that could help the traumatized city all night long. Bob was exhausted, but elated by the role his station had played in helping thousands of bewildered listeners. Bob looked fondly at the historic tower, and then stepped around the door to survey the last tower, Tower C.

He gasped in dismay. The top third of Tower C lay against the fence hundreds of yards away, apparently snapped and carried by a tornado.

Bob White gazed sadly at the towers with more than a little despair and regret. Those towers were not just *any* old radio towers. All had been built before WWII and were three of only six towers with their unique diamond design that still stood in the USA, three of only nine that remained in the entire world. Or *had* remained....Now two of them lay like twisted corpses on the field, beheaded by a consuming enemy. Those historic towers had had an almost mythical history, and a range that no one could quite believe. At night, WBT-AM could be heard from Cuba to Canada! The towers had to be rebuilt, and had to be rebuilt exactly. But how? Bob White had scoured the archives. There were no blueprints. Where would he find an engineer that could rebuild ancient towers of such a unique geometry *without plans?* But there was no question; they must be rebuilt.

*****

An engineer watched the storm howling outside his window. His head leaned against his shoulder, cradling the phone as he glanced through the new tower specs. The distraction of the storm and the tower blueprint did not dull his excitement listening to the voice of his beloved. He would never have foretold the destructive tempest that swirled in his future, listening now to the comforting breeze of her words.

CHAPTER THREE
A Towering Love
Early August 1989

Tony Fonseca's work on a tower in Florida was done for the day. He clapped the construction manager on his clammy sweat-soaked back, and said, "Time for a cold shower! See you tomorrow." Tony had worked all day in the sweltering heat. The tropical wave that would one day become the monstrous Hurricane Hugo would soon begin to form a few thousand miles east of him. For now, there was no forecast of any worries, no threats on the radar. No one suspected the massive storm that would shatter so many lives was just two months in the future. In fact right now, the air was perfectly still, heavy with humidity. Tony unbuckled his safety gear and carefully repacked it in the duffle bag. While glancing up at the tower, he gratefully removed the hardhat, shaking drops of sweat from his dark curls, now plastered against his forehead. The sun glinted off the metal and a large bird circled on the thermals above the tower. It had been a good day's work, but hot. A shower would be a blessing.

Tony went to dinner alone, as he always did unless he was entertaining a customer. Tony loved people, and loved to talk. However, he did not mind these solitary dinners. His work was rewarding, and exhausting. The peaceful time of solitude afforded him time to reflect on what he had done, and on what remained to be done. He had first gone to the hotel exercise room, when work ended. Tower work could be very tiring, particularly if he was climbing a tall tower; but it was not like the aerobic workout on a bicycle or a run. In the eight years since graduating from the Citadel, he had not gained a pound. It felt good to be young, strong, and fit. Now, having pedaled for an hour, showered, and reinvigorated, he ran a hand through his damp hair and perused the menu.

"Would you like a drink, sir?" asked the waitress.

"Just water thanks... it's a hot one out there!"

The waitress smiled, "It's always hot. You get used to it."

"I guess you can get used to anything," he said smiling.

The waitress smiled back as she left the table. A nice man, she thought. Respectful, genuine, considerate. And, she noticed, no ring on his finger.

When his food arrived, Tony devoured the flounder. He never ate red meat, health conscious and determined to remain strong and fit. He leaned back against his chair, thinking over the day at the tower. His mind was rarely still. Involved in every aspect of the tower construction, he was always plotting how he could simplify the process, engineer parts such that the riggers could work more safely, more quickly. He sipped his water, remembering the view from atop the spire -- the cloudless blue sky with the thick humid air barely moving about him, the distant horizon with layers of blues and greens. The sun was so persistent that the metal of the tower burned to the touch. He always wore gloves, despite the sweat that pooled around his fingers. Yes, it had been uncomfortably hot, but it was always a little cooler sitting on top of the world. He thought, not for the first time, that he loved his work.

Tony signed the credit card slip for his dinner, and thanked the waitress. She beamed back at him, and wondered why the young handsome man was eating alone. Tony headed past the bar lounge area. He was not much of a drinker, but a beer seemed like a pleasant cap on the torrid day. As he took his beer from the bartender, he noticed two women at a nearby table, having a drink. They were laughing over some shared story, and glanced up, mirth dancing in their eyes as Tony walked by. He smiled and said, "Hello," sitting down at the table next to them. They were friendly, and not immune to the attention from the charming young man. Soon the three of them were chatting and trading stories.

One of them in particular struck Tony's fancy. Mara was attractive, slender, and good natured. She was open and easy to talk to. She was so pleasant, and personable that soon they exchanged phone numbers and made a date for dinner the next evening.

Over the next few months, Tony and Mara visited each other back and forth between Florida and South Carolina. Tony was in the first blush of this blossoming relationship when Hugo roared through and snapped the WBT-AM towers.

Early in the relationship that had quickly become serious, they travelled with friends to the Bahamas. Mara had lived in the Bahamas at one time, and during that trip, made a comment that gave Tony pause. She talked about one day moving there, but there was a subtle undertone that Tony was not to be a part of this future plan. It was hard for Tony to put his finger on exactly what bothered him about the comment, but he felt hurt. Something about the way she said it made him feel that those future plans were not to include him. Yet they had talked about a future together. He was uncomfortable and uneasy but ignored his concerns. Surely he was overreacting.

Mara moved to Columbia for the summer, to see how things between them would proceed. Tony was becoming increasingly attached to Skylar, Mara's son from her first marriage. Her first husband had died tragically. Tony knew that the relationship with Mara was at a point where marriage was the next logical step. He had some concerns that there were already dramatic highs and lows. The highs he expected, with this new romance. The lows disturbed him. He remembers, in retrospect, explosive misunderstandings that took him by surprise. While he felt marriage was the right thing to do, and what he wanted, he also felt that circumstances were rolling over him and he was being pulled along. There were rumbles of concern, but he didn't listen to them. He loved Mara, he loved Skylar; he had a good job, and felt this was 'the one.' It seemed right, so he buried the concerns and asked Mara to marry him. As he slipped the diamond ring on her finger, he squashed the undercurrent of worry.

Collapsed tower after Hugo - photo Ted Bryan

CHAPTER FOUR
A Towering Mess

Only a handful of the diamond shaped towers had ever been built by the Blaw Knox tower company, out of business since the 1950s. The exact number of diamond towers that had at one time existed was unknown, but now only nine remained in the entire world. All nine of the remaining Blaw Knox towers had the distinctive diamond design. All came to a tapered point at both ends and had a middle rectangular section. One of the engineering wonders of the world was the ten inch ceramic base that held the weight of those towers.

In the United States, one tower stood in Cincinnati, one in Nashville, and one in Columbus. The other three were in Charlotte. The WBT-AM "sticks" were the only cluster of Blaw Knox towers. 'Skinny sticks' were the straight uniform width guyed towers that most people are familiar with. The second common tower design is the free standing or self-supporting tower, with a triangular or square wide base that rises to a tapered top.

Even most tower builders are not aware of the Blaw Knox design. They were so rare and had been constructed for such a limited time, that many modern engineers had no idea they had ever existed. Hungary had the tallest diamond tower in the world, an imposing 1031 feet high. In fact the tallest structure in Hungary was at one time, that Blaw Knox tower. All the Blaw Knox diamond towers had been built in the 1930s and 40s.

Blaw Knox was no longer in business, though some of its products had been acquired by Ingersoll-Rand. Blaw Knox road pavers were still produced. Without blueprints of the towers, the original builder no longer extant, and the towers in such a crumpled mess, Bob White, the chief engineer, knew it would be a challenge finding someone willing to tackle the rebuild.

Very little is known or written about Blaw Knox towers. The few people that bother to write about them, however, really love them. The company records with the original engineers' designs and motivations were all lost in a company fire. No one knew why the unusual design had ever been built, or why so few had been constructed. It was a unique and effective design. All the Blaw Knox towers that remained had an incredible range. None were perhaps as spectacular as the WBT-AM array's signal, however. The engineers could not lose that range, which stretched from Cuba to Canada, sometimes further depending on atmospheric conditions.

Bob and Ted walked out onto the field together the day after the storm and began to develop their strategy. The first decision was: replace or rebuild? The skinny uniform width tower design was more economical, and most engineers felt it was as good a transmitter as the Blaw Knox. Ted and Bob bristled at the idea. There was no denying that the range of their towers was (or had been) spectacular. While there had been a few attempts to demonstrate objectively the superior transmitting capacity of the diamond design, there was no definitive proof of that. In fact, Ted had come to the conclusion that the towers were originally built because the design was pretty. Still, as he and Bob looked at their injured towers, he could not quite shake the nagging desire to put them back just as they had been. They were indeed pretty, but they also had been a part of WBT-AM for most of its history. And besides, what if they lost the near miraculous range by replacing them with uniform width towers?

How could they justify the cost of the rebuild, even assuming they could find an engineer willing to do it? Bob had a solution.

"If we rebuild with the skinny guyed tower, we would have to redesign all our broadcast equipment. Replace all of it," said Bob.

Ted knew this was true. The equipment itself would be the same type, but manufacturers design for specific parameters. The equipment would need a different range than what the Blaw Knox equipment had. And new equipment would be costly!

He eagerly pursued this rationale in support of rebuilding the beloved Blaw Knox. Were they to build uniform width towers, it would have been an additional $75,000 to replace the broadcast equipment alone. In addition, they would have to do a complete engineering study of "proof of performance" to replace the towers, but only half of that were they to rebuild the towers exactly. The two engineers researched, and conspired. In the end, they felt they could justify a rebuild, with the whole project estimated to run a half million.

"Of course we will call Kline Towers," said Bob

"No question," said Ted.

*****

The towers stand on a 17-acre field. Nowadays, as then, there is nothing in the field but the tower support buildings and a huge expanse of grass. There is one enormous boulder that could not be removed when the towers were built. A large underground array of wires radiate from the towers, although for the portion of the field where the boulder juts, the wires criss-cross on its exposed surface.

In the 50s and 60s, WBT-AM had a herd of goats that 'mowed' the grass. Then a trailer park went up next to the field, and the residents killed the goats. In fact, the residents of the trailer park were in general unsavory characters that made life for the engineers difficult. Several of the trailer park residents operated methamphetamine labs and the engineers would often be shot at as they entered the transmitter building.

During that time period, engineers were on site 24 hours a day to man the station by the tower. The tower array and support equipment required constant maintenance. In the mid 1970s, it became remote controlled and they no longer needed to be continually on site. This was a relief to the engineers who dodged bullets to get into the building. It was not usually an issue during the day, but at night the dangerous characters came out like cockroaches. There still remain bullet holes in one door to a storage room in the building.

The transmission equipment became smaller over the years reducing the need for the full building space. Where huge computers and transmitters used to take up entire rooms, memorabilia and archival documents were now stored.

A bomb shelter was built in the basement by the Federal government during the Cuban Missile Crisis. It is still stocked with rations from that time period, as well as housing an old generator should the station lose power. In that period of deep concern over the threat of communism and nuclear holocaust, WBT-AM would transmit regular programming during the day, but at night, the government would take control of the station and transmit propaganda.

Fear mounted that the station could become a target should the crisis escalate. That fear of enemy attack was not new to the station. During WWII, the station had been similarly concerned. In fact, a rotating red aircraft beacon had been erected on the roof of the transmitter building at that time. No one knew why it was there, but most theories postulated worry of attack by the enemy. This made little sense to me and was the first spark of what became an obsession to solve the beacon mystery.

Jerry Dowd, the current chief engineer, speculated early on that it was there to prevent snipers or enemy attack, though nothing in the log books or archives alluded to its purpose or its installation date. It was a long standing mystery that many had speculated about, but never solved.

Following the discussion with Bob, Ted contacted Kline Towers, and two other companies. One company flat out refused to rebuild without plans, and the second agreed to consider the near impossible rebuild but at an exorbitant rate that WBT-AM could not afford. Kline Towers agreed to send an engineer the week after the storm.

Bob headed back to the main office, and Ted walked across the transmitter field back to the building. The lot next to the station where the rowdy and dangerous drug dealers lived was now blessedly quiet. Tall weeds grew, giving cover at night to the addicts who squatted and took potshots at the engineers.

Ted skipped up the granite steps of the transmitter building. He glanced at the molding above the door where an old Marconi microphone, the iconic symbol of a radio station, was carved in bas relief.

As he opened the door, he walked by a spare tower beacon. The sunlight glinted off of the Fresnel lens. It was the Federal Lighthouse Bureau that had first designed the lens that would eventually be used in tower beacons. When lighthouses were first built, they only had oil lamps. The Fresnel lens was designed to maximize and magnify the small amount of light so it could be seen at a great distance.

Now Fresnel lens strobes were much smaller and lighter than the old ones. In fact, they are so much more powerful that the FAA no longer requires that towers be painted red and white in the locations where the powerful strobe lights are used. Like the lawn mowing goats, the era of red and white towers is no longer relevant.

Ted walked by the black panels along a wall, the old 50,000-watt transmitter. It would only be used in dire circumstances but is even today fully operational. It was added in the 1980s.

Nowadays, the station has a brand new state of the art 50,000-watt transmitter. However, its function remains the same as the older transmitter present at the time when Ted was an engineer at WBT-AM. In the daytime, it channels power to the B tower. At night time, it divides power to the other two towers as well. Of course, with towers A and C knocked down by Hugo, only B was functional. The FCC did not want the station to drag its feet getting the damaged towers back online.

In daytime, the station is nondirectional. This means only one tower is used, Tower B, which broadcasts in all directions. This was critical for WBT-AM as to the west was the important suburb of Gastonia, a huge potential customer base. At night, the station normally switches on all three towers and the signal becomes directional. Directional means that two or more towers are used, with one as a broadcast tower, and the others to block the signal from going in an undesired direction. The station can thereby control where the beam is directed and can obtain a larger broadcast range in one desired direction. In the case of WBT-AM, the broadcast direction is north/south when it goes directional. Ted remembered there had been reports of German u-boats off the Carolina shore in WWII listening to WBT-AM at night, a tribute to its remarkable range even when omnidirectional. Bob White, a WWII buff with a special interest in submarines, had read a book called Operation Drumbeat, which was the diary account of a German submarine captain. In the book, the captain specifically mentions sitting off the coast of North Carolina in his submarine, listening to WBT-AM Christmas carols. He and his entire crew were singing along with the WBT-AM broadcast.

Following Hugo, with towers A and C down, the station remained omnidirectional day and night. The station owners were happy with this arrangement as it increased their range even at night to include the important listener base of Gastonia. Unfortunately, that worked against Bob and Ted's vision of resurrecting their towers. The station was in no hurry to lose Gastonia again, but the FCC was wearying of complaints from an Omaha, Nebraska station whose signal was being interfered with at night by the incredible transmission range of Tower B. So the station managers were dragging their feet on approving the tower reconstruction, while the FCC was haranguing Bob to get moving on the project.

A radio signal can be thought of as a big balloon surrounding the tower. If one side were pushed in, the balloon would bulge out on another side. With the directional towers blocking the signal to the west, the signal to the east over the ocean could certainly be expanded. Of course, WBT-AM wouldn't want to do that with the Atlantic Ocean only 100 miles east. Why broadcast to fish?

Ted Bryan beside base insulator - Photo by Vicky Kaseorg

So calls were made to Kline Towers, and preliminary arrangements made for an engineer to come see the crippled towers. Now Ted went down the stairs to the old bomb shelter. Maybe the tower blueprints were down here somewhere. It would certainly make the job of rebuilding easier if he could get his hands on the blueprints. He glanced at the emergency generator in an adjoining room that the government had given the station during the Cuban missile crisis -- a six-cylinder diesel Cummins Generator set.

During the hurricane itself, they had fired up the old Cummins when power went out. Unlike every other station in the path of the hurricane, WBT-AM stayed on, thanks to the Cummins.

Ted opened every drawer and cabinet in the storage area, both in the basement and then on the main floor. There was equipment stashed in every corner, as well as old logs and boxes of archival information strewn all about the building. Ted looked everywhere. No blueprints.

When he had contacted Kline Tower, he had of course warned them there were no blueprints. Still, he had hoped he might find them. Ted didn't quite know how the engineer would rebuild without them, but Kline was sending him in the morning. The station managers had at least agreed to let Kline look at the towers and give an estimate to rebuild. If only they had the blueprints! If only Blaw Knox were still in business!

As Ted locked the building and headed to his car, he heard the hawk screech. He glanced up and saw the hawk perched on the mysterious beacon, with a quizzical expression on his cocked head.

CHAPTER FIVE
A Towering Purpose

The hawk was not the only one with questions. I had an inexplicable desire to solve the beacon mystery and went after a solution with a vengeance. My brother, a radio fanatic, had sent me on a field trip eight years ago to the towers. While my radio knowledge was limited to plugging one in, John felt I was the one for his assignment: take pictures and learn all I could about the towers.

Ted Bryan, retired by then, had graciously shown me the station and the towers, and mentioned the mystery of the beacon. As soon as I learned that no one knew why it was there, I began to wonder. How could this mystery be unsolved for seventy years? WBT-AM was a major radio station with an important past. Why was there no record of this historic beacon's purpose? It seemed to me the best place to start would be with any connection of the towers to the war, since most agreed the beacon was installed during WWII.

I was surprised to discover that Blaw Knox Towers have a rich history in WWII. I eagerly pursued this lead, desperate to uncover some clue in that history that suggested why the WWII era beacon was on the WBT-AM transmitter building.

The mystery completely captivated me. How could such an interesting, ancient beacon be in such a public place for such a long time, and yet no one knew why it was there or what its purpose had been? Some people had suggested it was to light the towers. The engineers at WBT-AM told me it made no sense that it would have lit the towers in the role of an obstruction beacon. The towers had always been well lit by beacons on the towers themselves. They felt it must have had some other function, but they had no idea what that might have been. There were no records or documents at all that provided any clues as to why the beacon was there, or by whom or when it was installed.

Obviously for seventy years no one had cared enough to dig very deeply. Like the WWII soldiers now in their 90s and dying off along with their stories, perhaps that beacon had its own fascinating tale of our country's history, something that might be a loss should it never be told. Like many unknowns, it is hard to contemplate what their importance might be until they are solved. I had no idea when I started my hunt for a solution what a fascinating history of the United States would be revealed just by following the distant beam of a now darkened, forgotten beacon.

Blaw Knox towers had varied roles in WWII, it turns out. One of the more interesting connections involved the diamond cantilevered tower used by WLW Cincinnati, built by Blaw Knox in 1933. It stretches an impressive 747 ft. into the air and is 35 feet wide at the midsection. The tower, which still stands, was originally over eight hundred feet tall, but was shortened for optimal broadcast capability. This tower is the second longest operating AM tower in Ohio.

WLW Cincinnati was distinctive in radio history for being the first station to use a directional antenna system. Originally started by Powel Crosley, and known as 'The Nation's Station,' WLW had a tremendous range. WLW could be heard in Europe and in the Pacific. A lookout tower was built for protection of the facility during WWII. On top of the tower was a spotlight, and guards were able to watch over the entire compound. There was apparently grave concern that WLW would be sabotaged, due to its role in disseminating propaganda during the War. It is rumored that the WLW transmitter was used to dispense coded communications. Some listeners at the time reported programming which was then interrupted with a ludicrous string of senseless words, beginning with the word 'pelican' repeated three times. Hitler apparently referred to the WLW owner Crosley as the 'liar of Cincinnati.' While WLW's role in Allied communication has never been acknowledged or confirmed, it seems clear that it did play a role that displeased the Furhrer. WBT-AM also had a guard tower, probably built during the war years, atop its transmitter building. It was removed after the war.

Like the WLW tower, WBT-AM is a clear channel, directional tower. Clear channel means no other station in the vicinity operates on its frequency. Another powerful transmitter, it has the potential during emergency situations to reach vast geographical areas. As with Cincinnati's WLW, the government has shown a good deal of interest in WBT-AM, both historically and currently. WBT-AM was just recently added to an elite list of AM towers that are a part of the Emergency Alert System (EAS) and Primary Entry Point (PEP) network. These stations are all considered transmitting powerhouses, and among other requirements, need diesel backup generators with the fuel and other self-sufficient support to transmit for thirty days continuously.

Ted Bryan, when showing me the support building at the WBT-AM tower site, had proudly pointed out the old diesel generator which had been given to the station by the government in the Cold War years, and was still operational. After explaining what it was, he had gazed at it with a respectful silence, as though waiting for me to bow my head in reverent awe. When I just blinked with massive lack of understanding, he sighed and moved on to other wonders of creation in the transmitter building.

The WWII-era beacon had been installed sometime around the war period on a low commercial building in no danger of being hit by aircraft. Was it to protect the towers, like the searchlight at the Cincinnati tower? The towers could conceivably have been used to transmit propaganda, though I had uncovered no evidence of that. The coded information reputed to have come out of Cincinnati had never been confirmed or denied either.

There were similar beacons atop other buildings of that era. The lovely art deco building in Chicago, now called the Palmolive building but once known as the Playboy Towers, housed a famous rotating beacon. Known as the Lindbergh Beacon, it was installed atop the building in 1930. There were two beacons originally. One was rotating, and helped planes navigate to Chicago. A second was stationary and pointed the way to the airport through coded flashes. In 1942, the beacon was extinguished. It was feared that the beacon would be used for navigation by invading forces during the Second World War! It is hard now to picture the hysteria that swept over this country after the bombing of Pearl Harbor. The war was 'over there.' However, even the Playboy club took time away from pinching bunny bottoms, fearing the enemy might be coming here, and took evasive action by extinguishing their famous beacon!

Blackout conditions were prevalent in Europe. Were there blackouts here as well? In the early decades of flight, visual aids were critical to the pilot. Might the beacon with its rotating red light have been necessary to help Allied pilots on their way to the front pinpoint flight position during blackout conditions? There were bases all along the east coast. Military airplanes patrolled the east coast, hunting for German submarines, as well as flying en route to Newfoundland, the jump-off point to Europe for American aviators.

During the early days of flying airplanes and calculating position, AM stations were actually used to help pilots 'triangulate' their location. These early radio navigation systems were employed by tuning to two different radio stations and then using a directional antenna to locate the broadcasting antennas. Plotting those two measurements on a map and graphing the intersection point assisted the pilot in determining his position. In fact, when a pilot was "flying on the beam," there was an audible hum. If he veered right or left, changes in the tone would alert him that he was off course. Commercial AM stations were useful for this application due to their tremendous range and power. This method of radio flying was still being used during WWII.

During that time, as now, the flashes of light on rotating aircraft beacons were color coded to indicate what sort of airstrip was present. For example, flashes of white-white-green would denote a military airport; white-green-red meant a hospital airdrome. The beacon with its rotating red light *could* help guide pilots in pinpointing their position at night if the world below them was dark and all lights extinguished, for fear of enemy attacks. Red light was less visible than white light, thus it could guide but not be seen as easily far away. It might help mark the position of the well-known WBT-AM radio tower as pilots overflew the station in the dark.

Rotating beacons were commonly used to guide planes in emergency or night conditions when it was difficult to fix their position visually. It seemed a possible role for the WBT-AM beacon.

The curator of a small vintage aircraft museum in Indiana, Atterbury-Bakalar Air Museum, kindly offered assistance. The museum housed many WWII memorabilia, including old WWII aircraft beacons. Jim, a docent at the museum, had been a top turret gunner on a B17 in Europe during the war. He asked me several questions and then said he knew a WWII pilot, John Walter, who could possibly help me.

John Walter, born February 19, 1921, was 91 years old when I spoke with him. He had flown 35 missions over some of the most hotly contested targets in Germany. He had had engines shot out during missions, and witnessed many injuries and deaths of crewmen from shrapnel. He had even written a book, My War, about his experiences.

After recounting the mystery of the WBT-AM Beacon, I proposed my theories of its purpose and waited for his applause. Instead, he gave me a history lesson. He was a much harsher critic of my theories than my dog had been.

"As you know, I am sure," he said, "there were blackout conditions in California after Pearl Harbor. In fact, I was an air raid warden at the time. My job was to go through the residential areas and make sure all the windows were covered. Street lights were off, and even the automobiles had to drive with only parking lights on. But I am guessing you know all that."

"And were there blackouts on the east coast as well?" I asked, deftly skipping over the need to affirm or deny the extent of my WWII knowledge.

"Yes," answered John, "In fact, German subs were sitting just off the coast. The lights from the coastline were silhouetting the tankers off shore, and the u-boats had perfect visible targets. They were sinking our ships right and left until we figured it out and had coastal black out conditions put in place."

"Would blackout conditions extend to Charlotte, just a hundred miles off the coast?"

"I doubt it," said John, "Not that far inland. Rotating beacons flash color codes to pilots. If there had been a green and white beacon flash, it would mean there was a landing strip right there. If it were red and white...."

"But my beacon is just red...I think...could it flash white too?"

"Yes, I am sure it did. And a red and white flash is like a finger pointing the pilot to a nearby airstrip to your Charlotte airport."

"Back then, pilots often flew by radio direction. They could mark position by triangulating radio signals. Could the WBT-AM towers have assisted pilots flying over the Atlantic during blackout conditions?" I asked.

"No," said John, "In fact, we were told specifically NOT to use radio beams to mark our position. The Germans were sending up false radio beams to confuse the pilots, and then they would shoot them down when they lured them off course."

While he acceded that if the command *not* to use the AM radio signals was issued, it was clear the pilots had at one time used them, John did not believe it was likely that WWII pilots had used WBT-AM nor the beacon light to navigate.

"Well if you couldn't fly using radio direction, how *did* you navigate over the Atlantic?" I asked, certain I would confound him.

"Two ways," John answered, "First, 'dead reckoning' and second, celestial navigation. With 'dead reckoning,' you determine air speed, wind direction and speed and put all that into a calculator, with knowledge of your start and anticipated end point, and you can reckon your position."

While the WBT-AM towers may or may not have been used by pilots, radio towers in other capacities *were* integral to success in WWII, where air superiority was critical to winning the war. Even the natives of Papua New Guinea, with no understanding of technology, recognized the critical role towers played in the War on the Pacific front. Their reverence was displayed by recreating fabricated wooden towers and life size airplanes made of sticks after the war ended, and the Japanese and Americans left the islands of the South Pacific. The Papuan New Guinea natives' curious *'Cargo Culture'* was born. In this strange adaptation to post-war life, they believed that these technological wonders which they could not begin to comprehend were created by deities. The natives believed that if they could reconstruct these wonders, perhaps the deities would shower material blessings once again on them. The natives, innocent bystanders of a war they had no interest in, built towers to symbolize the largesse of the Gods that had brought them so much material wealth along with the bombs.

Blaw Knox towers served another equally essential purpose in the War. They were among the towers that transmitted sorely needed morale boosting in the encouraging pronouncements of the 'Voice of America'. The Blaw Knox tower of WSL in Salt Lake City was heard as far as Australia during the war. The pilot John affirmed that the radio programs that were transmitted to Europe were a huge source of encouragement.

"They downplayed, or didn't mention the defeats, but they told us quite a bit about our victories. And they would transmit music, mostly the Big Bands. It was quite enjoyable to hear that, those memories of home so far away."

There was no doubt that WBT-AM could be heard in Europe at nighttime, when the atmospheric conditions were most conducive to long distance radio transmission. If the radio station could be heard, the signal could be used for navigation.

WSL played another crucial ongoing part in the war. The WSL Blaw Knox tower (Salt Lake City) had been built around 1933. It was 450-feet tall. The original 50-kW Western Electric 7A transmitter that the tower supported was removed in 1940 and taken over by the Office of War. It was to be used aboard a ship destined for Europe in WWII. The transmitter was originally to be installed on the Radio Ship Phoenix, and sent to Europe, but through a series of events, it ended up on the Radio Ship, Triton Maris. Triton Maris set off to the Pacific, and became one of the most utilized broadcast ships in WWII. The transmitter that had served the WSL Blaw Knox was now broadcasting in part to jam the Japanese radios, and in part to disseminate war propaganda to aid the allies in Australia, and the islands of the Pacific rim.

With the many connections between other Blaw Knox towers and WWII, it seemed more likely than not that the WBT-AM towers had a role as well. I felt certain that exploring that wartime role would ultimately shed light on the beacon mystery. I trolled the internet for other experts to harangue.

CHAPTER SIX
A Towering Legacy

A tower aficionado, Jim Hawkins, maintains a fascinating and informative web page that has compiled information on Blaw Knox towers. There is little information about Blaw Knox outside of Hawkins' page. Most of the information that follows came from his excellent web page.

Blaw Knox began in 1906 as the Blaw Collapsible Steel Centering Company. Its main product was a unique method of molding concrete for heavy construction. Prior to an invention by Jacob Blaw, concrete used for heavy construction was molded using wooden forms. His work was combined with pioneering casting methods using pressed and wooded steel developed by Luther Knox, combining the innovative geniuses in both steel and concrete construction. The new company was renamed Blaw Knox in 1917. Ten years later, radio towers were added to their product line. Several companies merged with Blaw Knox over the years, including some involved in road construction. Blaw Knox became the product name of a road construction paver, and is now part of the product line of Ingersoll Rand. Blaw Knox stopped producing towers in 1958, and went out of business some time after. There were no specifics about when the company had completely folded, but it appeared to have at least its paver product absorbed by Ingersoll Rand.

During the Great Depression, Blaw Knox remained profitable. It was during this time, in fact, that it erected the diamond shaped towers. It made other towers as well, of more traditional construction. Why did it make those diamond towers? Hawkins' site revealed no insights other than to say that no one really knows as all the records of the original engineers' ideas or rationale are gone, just as Ted Bryan had mentioned.

After the Depression, the Blaw Knox Company became pivotal in supporting Allied efforts in WWII. Blaw Knox cast armor for naval vessels, turrets for tanks, naval gun slides and mounts, rockets, projectiles, torpedo launching equipment and the operation of a 16-inch shell line, among other things.

During WWII, Blaw Knox also made antiaircraft Bofor gun mounts. The Bofor gun itself was made by a Swedish company. The Bofor antiaircraft gun was apparently crucial in the war against the Japanese aircraft. Commended for their war efforts, Blaw Knox had won several Army Navy "E" awards.

Kline Towers, like Blaw Knox, was renowned for its excellence, and for taking on unusual projects. Its reputation was stellar. Ted and Bob had known as soon as the station agreed to the rebuild that they would contact Kline.

In a TV, FM, or cell phone tower, the tower is the structure that supports the antennae. In an AM radio tower, the tower *is* the antennae. The structure and geometry is integral to the kind of signal, and range it transmits. Ted knew that WBT-AM towers had an incredible range, and no matter what the experts said about the lack of proof of superiority of the diamond design, he wanted his diamond towers back. That task seemed impossible, but Kline was known for doing the impossible.

Kline Towers began as a family business in the 1920s. At that time, they were not involved in tower building but in large steel construction, particularly platforms. Like Blaw Knox Company, Kline also had a role in WWII. They built bulkheads for the naval shipyard in Charleston. While Blaw Knox was building the armor for the naval ships, Kline was making them sturdy with watertight sections should that armor leak.

The war ended. Like Blaw Knox, Kline survived and thrived. In the 50s, Kline formed its tower division. From that early start, Kline Towers had always had the reputation of seeking unique projects.

Their reputation preceded them. Ted knew other companies were not eager to go off the beaten track, preferring the more profitable path of least resistance. But not Kline. The bigger the challenge, the more they shined. Ted called them, knowing that the little known Blaw Knox towers had the greatest chance of being successfully rebuilt by a company known for innovation and courage.

*****

October 1989

The chief engineer, nicknamed Skosh, walked over to Tony's desk. Tony was busy drafting a drawing of tower specifications. He drew slowly and carefully. He didn't notice his boss approach, so intent was he in finishing the line. The scent of the coffee drifting from the mug in the chief engineer's hand pierced his concentration and he looked up.

"Tony, we have a mess in Charlotte."

"We have a mess all over," Tony added, "Hugo really chewed us up and spit us out."

"I want you to look at those WIS towers up in Charlotte that we built. They need a structural analysis, see how well they handled the storm. But there is something else. You ever hear of WBT-AM?"

"Sure," said Tony, "they have a tremendous range. I've heard them in Miami."

"Hugo knocked down two of the three towers in their array. They are interesting towers -- cantilevered design. Really unique. Not many of them left. They want to know the cost to rebuild. I'd like you to take a look at them, if you are willing."

"Absolutely!" said Tony. He loved challenges, and the idea of a cantilevered tower interested him. He had been with Kline for seven years now. He could not recall seeing this cantilevered design ever before. He had worked on "skinny towers," the uniform width "sticks" that had guy wires pouring off them like porcupine quills. And he had worked on the triangular self supporting towers, with a wide base that tapered at the top. Why would anyone build a cantilevered tower?

Skosh handed him a photograph of the towers toppled by Hugo.

"That's interesting," Tony said, "They are kind of a mix of self supporting and guyed towers. Who made these?"

"Blaw Knox. Out of the tower business for decades now. The towers were built around WWII. This is the kicker, Tony...they don't have blueprints."

Tony looked at the pictures, already analyzing what he might need to do in rebuilding the towers. Skosh smiled. The fact that Tony seemed completely unfazed by the absence of blueprints was exactly why he had asked Tony to oversee the project.

The pictures taken after the hurricane showed the towers partially sheared and torn as though made of paper rather than steel. Tower A was a crumpled twisted mess of steel, the top half still attached at points to the bottom half, but lying on the field like a partially decapitated corpse. Tower B was intact, but the structural integrity could be compromised after such a fearsome knocking about. The top third of tower C was completely sheared off, and lay at the distant edge of the field.

"How soon do they want me to take a look?" Tony asked.

"Yesterday," laughed Skosh, "The two directional towers as you can see by that picture are out of commission. So the signal from that middle tower isn't blocked -- they are getting complaints of broadcasting interference from Nebraska."

"That's a pretty spectacular range," agreed Tony, "I gather Nebraska isn't too thrilled."

"They are motivated to have those towers fixed...just like they were. They don't want to lose that range."

Towers A and C were, as Tony's boss mentioned, directional towers. That meant that their purpose was to cancel the signal from going in a specific undesired direction (east and west in this case.) WBT-AM transmitted along a north-south line, so the directional towers were to the east and west of the middle transmitting tower to cancel any signal in that direction. During the rebuild, the FCC gave special dispensation to allow WBT-AM to broadcast omnidirectionally. They had no choice, unless they were to be shut down altogether. To placate the Nebraska station whose signal was now interfered with, WBT-AM dropped their transmission to 25,000 watts at night. Meanwhile, Ted and Bob anxiously awaited the verdict of the tower company with the reputation for taking on the challenges other companies wouldn't touch.

Kline Towers, in Columbia, South Carolina, was only ninety minutes from Charlotte. The very next day, Tony drove to Charlotte. Uprooted trees still dotted the drive, the aftereffects of Hugo. Power outages would remain for two weeks in many locations along the route, the devastation and debris much longer.

Ted Bryan met Tony as he pulled up to the gate at the transmitter field. He hopped out of the car and introduced himself eagerly, then looked over the field. Scattered limbs were still splashed across the grass outside the field. Some trees on the edge of the field, just beyond the fence were as mangled as the towers.

"Quite a sight, eh?" said Ted.

"The original engineers probably never expected a Charlotte tower to have to stand against a hurricane," said Tony, "Nice that the middle one managed to stay up."

"Providential," agreed Ted, "We haven't missed a broadcast moment yet."

"Pretty impressive!" remarked Tony, "So, what's the goal here? We could take these down and put up three skinnies. Probably more economical than a rebuild."

"Problem with that," said Ted, "is we would have to get a whole new configuration of support equipment. That's not cheap. If feasible, we really want the exact same array that we had."

"The cantilevered design?"

"That's right. Now you have your work cut out for you. You understand we have no blueprints."

Tony nodded, looking out over the field, assessing the challenge. Grabbing his camera from the seat beside him, he flung the strap over his neck and slammed the car door shut. A hawk sitting on the tower startled, and with a great flap of wings flew off to the nearby trees lining one edge of the field. It settled on a limb, strangely denuded of leaves from the hurricane, and watched the men across the field. Tony snapped a photograph. The camera was always with him, even when he climbed the towers.

Now he gazed at the broken towers, crumpled on the field, surrounded by the storm wreckage. The metal was twisted and contorted where it had half broken away on Tower A, the most severely damaged. Knowing he had no plans to guide him, he first had to measure and match each piece exactly. He could not use a mangled twisted piece to gather exact measurements. He looked up and down the middle tower. It was intact, and would be useful in measurements if it was exactly identical to the other two. However, in all likelihood, built many years apart, the pieces might not be identical. Thus Tony recognized that step one was to find undamaged pieces that he could use as templates for measuring. In his favor, the Blaw Knox tower was essentially four identical faces joined together. If he could find undamaged pieces anywhere on those four faces, he could reconstruct using intact pieces for measurement. And of course, to keep costs down, any steel parts that could be salvaged would be.

The towers, while tapered at both ends, had a vertical section in the middle. Tower A had collapsed under the square face piece, the vertical section. It was guy wired just under that vertical face. Tony thought about what he would need to do to insure the rebuilt towers matched, but also would withstand modern wind load standards. Towers are designed to withstand specific wind speeds average for the area. Of course, all bets are off when a hurricane comes through. Engineers *can* over-design, but it is usually not economically feasible.

"Shall we go in?" suggested Ted, unlocking the gate to the field, and interrupting Tony's thoughts.

"Yes," said Tony, "If we are lucky, we will find enough intact pieces that I can get accurate measurements. We will of course have to take that tower top apart, and bring it back to the factory."

"That's a lot of steel to be transporting," said Ted.

"In the end, it will be worth it," said Tony, "If we can reconstruct it at the factory we will know it will all fit when we get it back to the field. We can engineer all the parts right there, to match perfectly." They climbed into Ted's Bronco and bounced across the field. Ted veered around chunks of metal.

"It was some storm," said Ted, "Almost killed Bob, our chief engineer, when that tower came down."

Tony pointed to the top third of Tower C, lying in a mangled mess at the far edge of the field.

"I have never seen anything like that," he said, "It is like it was just ripped off by a giant and tossed like a baseball."

At the base of Tower A, they got out of the car. It was a warm day, typical for late September in North Carolina. The humidity was low, and a slight tinge of coolness in the breeze reminded them that fall was not far away. Cicadas hummed like background singers, not consciously noticed by the engineers. The blue sky could have been painted, so perfect and clear it was. A flock of birds in the trees at the edge of the field sang out in frenzied chorus, and then fell silent. Tony shielded his eyes, looking up to the point where the tower had collapsed. The entire vertical section and tapered top, everything above the guy wire, was twisted and crumpled. Tony walked slowly around the sheared top section. Ted followed him. Each time Tony found an undamaged brace, bolt, strut, or cross piece, he pointed it out gleefully. Despite extensive damage, it looked like on one or another of the identical faces, there might be enough intact pieces to measure what was needed. He wouldn't know that till he began careful labeling and reconstruction at the factory. Exact measurements would be critical. The bottom section was intact, so the top reconstructed section had to fit perfectly, with exactly the same measurements as the now mangled top.

"What about rebuilding it right here at the field?" asked Ted.

"We can't do that," mused Tony, "Since we are reconstructing every bolt, every piece, we need to be at the shop."

"What's your plan?" asked Ted, "That's a pretty big heavy chunk of scrap."

"We will take it apart, piece by piece," said Tony, "and transport it to the shop. I will make shop drawings there. I can draw out all the details, the connections...everything we need to fabricate the parts."

Tony was confident he could do so. Part of his training at Kline had been in structural steel detailing. For six months, he had learned how to exactly draw plans that showed the factory workers how to fabricate necessary pieces. With a project as unique as this one, that skill would prove to be invaluable.

"The first step will be to get a rigger in here -- take down the damaged section. Then, we will have to collect all the pieces, label them, and take them to Columbia." Tony knew this was easier said than done. The top section, still attached by shards of crumpled steel, was under enormous stress right now. Taking it down safely would be a challenge. At any moment it could all shear loose.

"That will be a few truckloads I imagine," said Ted, "Too bad Hugo couldn't be hired to carry it there."

Tony chuckled, running his hand though his thick curls, "That *would* be easier if it were possible. Personally, I'm kinda glad Hugo is gone. But we'll hire a rigger to come out here. Cut down the pieces up there." They all looked up, following Tony's gaze. The hawk had settled again midway up Tower B and glared at them, with its hooded eyes.

"You'll be able to rebuild it, just like it was?" asked Ted. He tried to keep the longing out of his voice.

"Yes," Tony assured him, "When we are done, you won't know it ever came down. This is a unique job to tackle. I would really like a go at it."

The hawk screeched and lifted up into the cloudless blue sky, so perfectly clear that it was hard to imagine a hurricane had ever dared smudge its surface.

*****

Tony was the second born of five children of a civil engineer who owned a construction business. Born February 7, 1959 in Utica, New York, Tony was employed from an early age in all aspects of his father's business. That section of upstate New York is rural, nestled in the foothills of the Adirondacks, rolling mountains with softly rounded tops. Thick forests surround green pastures, interrupted by small villages dotting the hillsides.

Utica is a small, industrial city, situated along the banks of the Mohawk River. It became a mill town, and a magnet for Italian immigrants. In fact, it became and to some extent still is, a center of organized crime, home to the infamous Cosa Nostra family. It is now a sleepy part of the nation, only sixteen-square miles with many of the major industries once there abandoning the harsh weather and high taxes for the south.

From youth, Tony had the heart of an engineer, long before the official degree was awarded to him. He was fortunate enough to be born to a family that could nurture his creative soul that wanted to build. Like many engineers, Tony spent his childhood taking things apart so he could figure out how they worked, and then putting them back together.

His father, also named Tony, was quite resourceful, saving money by fixing the inevitable breakdown of appliances and structures that every home-owner faces. He would sit young Tony down near him, and without fail, repair the broken item. Tony, young and energetic, remembers growing antsy at times.

"But I'm not doing anything!" he cried.

"Observe," gently admonished his father, "just observe."

Tony's father, though a U.S. citizen, spent much of his young life till adulthood in Portugal, thus had dual citizenship there. He returned to the United States to attend New York University for engineering. Upon graduation and beginning his career in New York, he corresponded with a Spanish girl he had been introduced to by a cousin. He travelled back to Spain with an engagement ring and paperwork for a marriage certificate, confident he could convince her to marry him. She was convinced, and the couple moved permanently to the United States.

Tony's mother spoke little English, though his father spoke three languages -- Portuguese, Spanish, and English. Thus, Spanish was the primary language Tony heard in the early years, and he was fluent in Spanish before English. He remains fluent in both languages.

His mother bore five children in seven years. Tony remembered fondly his early years, traveling often to

Spain to spend summers there with his extended family. His dauntless mother, with five small children in tow and little command of English, managed to safely navigate through the airports to bring her brood safely each summer to Spain. She recalls one trip putting the four month old baby in a cardboard box under her seat on the plane while her two-year-old sat on her lap, and her three-year-old beside her. Tony's father usually had to remain behind in America. He owned the construction business by then, and was building a stellar reputation in upstate New York.

Sara Maria Fonseca, Tony's mother was born in Spain on June 28, 1930. Her father was an attorney. Her mother died when Sara was only eight years old, and she remembers her father as being very close and loving. It was he that she credits with giving her the values and character that helped her raise her own five children.

"Every single one of them became a professional," Sara declared proudly, "The oldest became a dentist, the second was Tony, the third became an architect, the fourth a physical therapist, and the fifth an engineer with an MBA."

What was her secret to raising a whole brood of accomplished people who remain close to each other, and to her?

With her heavy Spanish accent, she quickly replied, "I tried to teach my kids right from wrong. And my husband was very strict. Nowadays people are so lenient! Let me give you an example. When Tony was young, and about to get his license, he took his brother, two years younger than he, and without permission took the car for a drive! Do you know what we did? We didn't let him get his license for a whole year because of that! We were always very stern. Better they cry than you cry, I always said!"

Tony's siblings mimic their mother's perception of why they all were raised so successfully. None ever got in trouble (much) except perhaps for the second boy, Gregory, whom they nicknamed "Pagan." All became successful professionals; all have grown children who also went on to success in college and careers. And all had stories of the legendary strictness of their father.

"We never ate out," said Maria Elena, the baby of the crew, "Every single bingle night we had to be dressed and ready for dinner. God forbid one should show up without a shirt or not properly dressed for dinner!"

"Nowadays," added Tony, "you can't spank kids without the threat of child abuse, but Greg and I got smacked a lot…more than the girls."

"But we all got the big wooden spoon. He would tell us to open our palms and he would whack us," said Roseanne, the fourth oldest.

He was a disciplinarian, always stressing education, always urging them all to work harder. Homework had to be completed before they could go to bed. And anyone who broke the father's rules faced his ire and the spoon.

"Now don't listen to them," urged Gregory, leaning forward, "I mean our dad *was* strict. But he was hardly abusive. He was a very loving father. We truly respected him, and we didn't want to disappoint him."

The Fonseca brood all echoed the same refrain. Tony Senior had instilled in all of them a sense of duty, honor, and honesty, as well as excellence. And he led by example. He never asked anything of them that he himself did not model.

The children all went to Catholic schools, segregated by gender until their high school days. Religion was integral to their life as a family. They all went to church every Sunday, recited the rosary together, and prayed together. They all felt that the deep spirituality, particularly of their mother was part of the glue that held them together as a family, and later as accomplished individuals.

The mother Sara now lives in New Jersey near Tony's two sisters, Sara the oldest and Rose Ann, the second youngest. Sadly, circumstances overcame the family and forced them out of Utica.

"We lost everything," Sara explained. Her husband had contracted a large roadway job and as in any development project, the city engineers provided the specifications regarding city pipelines, electric lines, etc. A geotechnical assessment, also provided by the city, gave specific soil and water conditions. Based on their assessments, Tony's father quoted his price, and began the work.

The geotechnical report was incorrect, and the construction hit water that flooded the site. Unexpected time and money was spent pumping out the water, resulting in his company going over-budget with huge loss of profits. Tony's father sued the city, and the case went to arbitration. He won, but by then, had lost everything. At the time, Tony was in college, and his parents told him little of what was happening, afraid he would quit college and return home to work and help them.

"And they were right," Tony said, "I would have."

Tony Senior moved his family to Connecticut where he partnered with his cousin on a condominium construction project. They built the condo development, and bought one themselves to live in. However, the economic climate shifted, the condos never sold, and once again, Tony Sr. lost every penny of profit. His cousin declared bankruptcy, but Tony Sr. was too proud and honorable to do so himself. He sold their home, and repaid the money owed. It was at this time that he was diagnosed with a devastating cancer. His second youngest daughter moved her parents to live with her in New Jersey. Two months later, Tony Sr. was dead.

"My faith is what sustained me," said Sara, "I could never have managed without faith."

Tony's mother still goes to church twice a day, every day. She often told him, "You have to have faith to believe, and you have to believe to have faith." That legacy of honor and faith so abundantly present in his parents made a lasting impression on the young engineer.

Tony's swarthy good looks are reminiscent of his heritage. His hair is curly with little receding hairline, and nearly black, even in his 50s.

"All natural," he proclaimed, smiling. Little if any grey was discernible, though he was pointing to the curls, not the color.

His dark eyes are accented by thick dark lashes and eyebrows, and contrasted with a brilliant white smile.

He has classic good looks -- a sharp, straight nose, firm jaw-line, tanned complexion, and fit, strong body. His eyes are kind, and his smile genuine. Warmth, sincerity, and good nature pour out of him. He is trim and muscular, not an ounce of fat on his fit physique despite being over fifty years old. He looks like a young man, fresh-eyed and eager. He has the air of someone who cannot wait to greet the day. His bountiful good looks are matched by a generous personality.

When his siblings were gathered, describing what a close knit family they had always been, Maria Elena paused and said, "We were always a close family, always made time to see each other. Well, except for Tony's defection."

He looked down a little sheepishly, but did not challenge Maria Elena's jab. In fact, he held out his palms in supplication and said in explanation, "You know, my mistake."

"Well it was not *all* his fault," Maria Elena admitted, "But he made a choice, and he chose to walk away from his family. He had a choice. You don't leave family."

Tony gazed at Maria Elena silently, the hurt of that terrible time washing over his face. I knew what episode was alluded to. It surprised me that he shouldered the blame without a word, knowing the forces that had pulled him in two utterly incompatible directions. There had been no *good* choice, and he had done the best he could. Rather than defend himself, he remained silent. However, that story was still in the future, long after Tony was approached by WBT-AM.

*****

Tony's father was critical in molding the man who would unabashedly take on the challenge of the rebuild.

"My Dad," explained Tony, "was very respected in his field. He was always honest and hard working, and prepared. I knew I wanted to be like my dad.

"And it was great. Every summer since I was old enough to hold a hammer, I worked with him. It was fantastic experience. I worked with masons, electricians, plumbers, iron workers.... in every single trade of commercial construction, I was gaining field experience. I always knew one day I would be a civil engineer. I thought I would work somewhere a few years first, then return to New York. I didn't just want to go work for my dad right off the bat, be handed something I hadn't earned just because I was his son. So I planned to work somewhere else and then go back...but I never did. Never did go back."

At first, he thought about entering the military. He wanted to serve his country. Part of that desire was patriotism, and part was that it would be wonderful to let the army pay for his education. His plan was to graduate, be a military engineer a few years, then return to work for his father. He discovered that to go to a military academy, he needed a congressman or some official to nominate him. Unsure of how to go about that, he found that if he attended The Citadel in South Carolina, no nomination would be required.

"So I went to The Citadel. Anyway, I was offered the 'advanced contract' where they pay two years of your tuition, and you work two years for the government when you get out. But my Uncle Jim and Dad talked me out of that. I could go to the Citadel four years, pay my way, and graduate with a civilian engineering degree. So that is what I did.

"My first job was with Kline Iron and Steel Company. I had a few interviews and I would always make sure I studied and learned all about the companies first. I researched Kline and I knew it was a company I would want to work for. Funny thing is when they interviewed me, I think I ended up asking more questions than they did! They called me back for a second interview."

Tony paused and shook his head, "Kline Towers was the best place for a new graduate to work. I mean, there I was, brand new and young, and no matter where I was sent on those early jobs, I was granted instant respect. Kline had such a stellar reputation that just being a Kline engineer, I could go anywhere in the world and people immediately respected my work. Of course, I earned respect too, but it was so much easier working for a company like that."

An engineer willing to tackle a rebuild like the Blaw Knox towers without any blueprints had to be fearless. What forces had molded someone who felt he could conquer the world when the odds were so against success?

"Well when I went to the second interview, they had the notes from my interview at The Citadel. I asked them, 'So, how did I do on my first interview?' The interviewer told me that they had written two words on my interview sheet – 'positive, and well-prepared.' Attitude makes all the difference."

One of Tony's inspirations is Chuck Swindoll. He keeps a Swindoll book on his desk in the office at his home. A guiding principle of Tony's life is to keep a positive attitude and he often quotes a favorite Swindoll verse:

"The longer I live, the more I realize that the impact of attitude on life...is more important than money, than giftedness...we have a choice on the attitude we embrace every day. We cannot control our circumstances...but we can play on the one string we have -- and that is our attitude."

Later, Tony's daughter mentioned that he always had a quote or a saying on his lips, always at the ready, to instruct and encourage. Usually, he said it in Spanish.

Kline Towers took the young engineer from The Citadel under wing. The first thing they did was put him in the "shop" where he learned all aspects of the nuts and bolts of the business. Similar to his experience with his father, the company understood that every cog in the company wheel was critical.

"I don't think many companies do that these days," said Tony, "When I started at Kline, they trained me from the bottom up. I worked in the plant on the steel floor, in the factory for six months. I learned the people, the procedures, the equipment, the bench marks and elevations for every piece of equipment...every aspect of our business. From what I know, that was very unique to Kline. It was all very comfortable to me -- I mean I had worked in every area of construction with my dad for all those summers. So when I saw those WBT-AM towers and knew I would have to rebuild without plans, well I wasn't concerned. I knew I could do it.

"I thought building and designing things was so cool! Now I sound like a kid, don't I? But you can probably tell I am really passionate about what I do. I mean, it is so rewarding to design something and then see it being built. With Kline, I could design the foundation, then I could go in the field, watch the concrete poured, and see it all assembled. Kline was unusual in that I could see the whole process, from conception to end of what I made. I didn't just design it and sit in an office. I actually was a part of the whole project. It was very creative. And the broadcast industry is great -- very interesting, caring people.

"The people who actually put up the towers, they are called 'erectors' or 'installers.' Anyway, if they had ideas, we would listen to them, and then go and change our design. We collaborated and incorporated their thoughts into our designs. Everyone in the whole place was valued. Even the so-called 'lowest' positions -- those people were geniuses in their own environment."

Much later, I would learn about a horrific tower collapse. Had an engineer listened to the concerns of the erectors and modified the design of a simple piece, that tower might never have fallen. Five young men might have lived to see wives and children one day. Tony rarely mentioned how dangerous his work was or how unique he was, not only in his background but in his concerns for the opinions of every worker, and also in climbing the towers he designed. Few engineers did that.

"I was surrounded by great people, a great team. At Kline, the owners never said someone worked *for* them...we all worked *with* them. You know, when I see a cashier, I always think, she has to work for a living just like I do. She is working just as hard as me to put food on the table, but so many people look down on what they call menial jobs. I always try to treat those folks with respect. Why should they be worthy of any less respect than me? I tell my daughter all the time, you don't need all these laws and rules and things to live by. You don't need the Ten Commandments or the Constitution...I mean those are great, but all you need is one thing -- to treat others the same as you want to be treated.

"We were called the 'Cadillac of the tower industry.' Our towers and our engineers were the most respected in the business." His pride and enthusiasm for Kline was infectious. Kline was clearly a remarkable company and had hired a remarkable man. Now the paths of this ingenious builder, historic towers, and an iconic radio station were about to intersect.

CHAPTER SEVEN
A Towering Re-creation

Flatbed Truck With Tower Pieces - courtesy Ted Bryan estate

Unfortunately, it was eight months before that long awaited intersection of tower with builder transpired. Despite Bob White and Ted's eagerness to restore the Blaw Knox array, the powers that be at WBT-AM were not unhappy to drag their feet on the rebuild. The station was content to have the middle tower transmit omnidirectionally as long as they could get away with it. The FCC was breathing down Bob's neck, wondering when the project would begin, and his managers were urging him to delay!

Bob and Ted were eager to have the tower array restored, but with the delay were able to give their bosses adequate financial rationale to do so. Finally in May of 1990, the scrap metal was cut down and the rebuild was officially begun.

It was with great satisfaction that Ted watched the two huge flatbed trucks rumble away, heading to I-77 South with the massive mangled tower bits lashed down. Tony had overseen the crew that dismantled the top half of Tower A, amputating the ruined metal piece by piece.

Arthur S Tower Company would be the tower erection team, under Tony's direction. Before they could begin, the Association of Mechanical Erectors arrived with a sixty ton crane to be used in cutting down the damaged section.

This was a particularly dangerous procedure. The foreman allowed no one else to climb the tower and cut away the broken sections. If someone had to die, it would be him...particularly since the crew was comprised of his three sons. First, both Tony and the foreman analyzed where the points of stress were, and which way the broken piece was most likely to fall when shredded metal connections were severed completely. If they miscalculated, the rebound could be deadly. While the crane pulled in one direction, the foreman cut away the damaged struts with an acetylene torch.

His wife, the company bookkeeper rarely was on site, but the afternoon that he cut away the dangling tower pieces, she stood below the entire time and prayed. The foreman later told Bob White that those prayers were responsible for keeping him alive and safe during this procedure wrought with danger.

As each piece was lowered to the ground and then loaded on the truck, Tony clambered over the sections, measuring and calculating. He would take measurements again in the shop. There would be no guess work. Every piece had to be recreated exactly, or the reformcd top section would not fit on the remaining bottom half. Every nut, bolt, connector plate, brace, and beam would have to be measured, drawn, and then manufactured at the shop.

Ted was happy to see the ruined tower pieces carted away. To him, it was just scrap metal, in the way. Once it was gone, the rebuild could begin. He did not feel any particular attachment to the metal carcass. The spirit of his towers remained, and he was anxious to resurrect a healthy body as soon as possible.

"You're sure the blueprints are gone, right?" asked Tony, as he surveyed the tower, "I mean sometimes prints get stored in the transmitter building."

"We looked," said Ted, "several times. I have scoured the whole place for them. They have disappeared."

"It's ok," Tony assured him, "It would just be a little less time consuming if we had the drawings."

"I can look again," Ted said. While the twisted metal was slowly piled on the flatbed, Ted dipped back into the transmitter building. He opened all the possible drawers (again) where the blueprints might be stashed for the third or fourth time, but as he expected, came back empty handed. He shrugged as Tony glanced up, his phone against his ear. Ted stuck his thumb downward.

Tony laughed, and shot his thumb up in return. He would not even regard the lost blueprints as a set-back, just an inconvenience. He ended the call, and patted his pocket.

"That's why I brought this," he said, pulling out the tape measure, "And when we're done, you'll have blueprints."

"Good," Ted told him, "Then we'll be ready for the next hurricane."

Temporary guy wires were stretched and secured onto the lower part of Tower A. A visual inspection indicated the tower was safe and the wires likely undamaged, but it was best to be certain with the temporary guys until new stress tests could confirm the tower's integrity. The Blaw Knox guy anchors were far superior to modern guy anchors. Nonetheless, Tony would never gamble with the life of any tower worker. Better safe than sorry.

Tony and the construction crew slowly walked around the base of the tower, looking for any visible signs of damage, buckling, or weakened metal. When the temporary guys were firmly anchored, Tony eagerly donned his safety equipment. He threw the camera strap over his neck and then settled the hard hat over his curls, smashing them down as he buckled the hat.

Climbing the Blaw Knox tower was a different experience than he was used to. Since the bottom half rose from a tapered base only a few inches wide to the fatter middle section, he was climbing with a different center of gravity than on any tower he had climbed before. He was careful, as always, to snap the lanyard on the tower every few inches. Tony was always careful, but rarely fearful. Still it is not easy for a bystander to forget that tower climbing is anything but routine work. The climber, particularly one scaling a tower of questionable integrity, is always trusting narrow braces to remain underfoot while gravity continues to tug and lure, a siren call that if succumbed to, can mean skulls splashing open like melons hitting the distant ground.

But Tony was not thinking of skulls smashing open. He was focused as he worked his way slowly up the outward slanted side, like a fly scaling the wall. Along the way, he paused frequently, carefully looking over the struts and braces, and visually scanning for any potential points of weakness. A structural analysis would be done using a computer program called STADD, to further assess the structural integrity. The computer would analyze joint loads, geometry of the structure, and the tower's ability to handle the stresses of any equipment that would need to be reinstalled. As Tony crawled up the side, he saw a hawk circle above Tower B, and then settle on a cross beam. It peered at him, with its unblinking piercing eyes. Ted had noticed the hawk showed up every day, always watching the rebuild proceedings.

"Don't worry," Tony told the hawk, "We'll get your perch back up soon enough."

When he reached the point at which the top section had sheared off, he tied on and rested. He pulled the lens cap off his camera and took several photographs.

Ted, constantly on site during the entire process, was nearly two hundred feet below him, shielding his eyes and gazing up. Tony snapped a picture of Ted, and then viewed the scene around him. He could see downtown Charlotte to the northwest, some five or ten miles away. The hawk sat nearly directly across from him now. Its head darted to the left, its laser stare directed at a distant movement in the grass below. From his perspective high atop the damaged tower, Tony spotted several trees downed by the hurricane, still sprawled across the distant fields.

Pulling out his tape measure and notepad, he began measuring. Tony needed exact measurements of the angles and lengths of each intact piece. At the shop, a connector piece would be fashioned to attach the intact base to the rebuilt top section. If Tony's calculations were off at all, the connector piece wouldn't fit. As Tony measured and sketched initial drafts that would be used to recreate the missing blueprints piece by piece, the hawk watched him.

*****

It felt like a party as the mangled steel parts were brought to the Columbia factory. The shop crew gathered, scrutinizing the massive chunks of scrap metal.

This is what happens to a tower," said Tony, "when it meets a hurricane."

With the torn and tangled steel pieces now laid out on the factory floor, Tony and the shop technicians began labeling and measuring the parts they would need

Worker atop tower piece -- Photo Ted Bryan estate

to fabricate. This was a laborious process. Every single bolt across all four faces of the tower had to be recreated. That meant, if possible, the crew had to find one undamaged bolt of each kind. The same was true of every beam, coupling plate, and connector. The length, width, angle, and thickness had to be determined for every piece, large and small, of the entire top half of the tower. In a sense, Tony was creating the blueprints for each small unit that comprised the whole, as well as the blueprint ultimately of the entire structure.

This initial step in and of itself might have stymied most tower engineers. Not Tony. For six to eight months, early in his training at Kline, Tony had been taught structural steel detailing. That meant he had learned everything he needed to know to make shop drawings showing the intricate details and connections necessary to fabricate the parts. Many engineers would not have had this kind of training. Tony's background was perfectly matched to the daunting task at hand. He was well versed in every single aspect of the tower construction and erection.

He rarely felt the need to sleep. He was completely energized and alive with the challenges of this project. And to add to his abundant creative energy, the relationship with Mara was still in the exultant throes of new romance. He called her every night, overflowing with the excitement of this unique work and his burgeoning love. His already enthusiastic delight with life felt like it would burst out of him. As the drawings of the tower parts began to slowly and meticulously coalesce, the lives of Tony and Mara began merging closer and closer.

While the pieces of the tower were being forged, Tony carefully compiled his measurements and drawings which would be used to create the blueprint of the whole tower. Each part was unique to the tower, and had to be specifically detailed and formed. Tony had a remarkable grasp of both the excruciating detail needed and the overall result. He had a clear sense of the steps needed to reach the goal, and never felt that the final product would fail. He never lost focus -- neither of the tiniest nut or bolt measurement, nor of the final unique geometry of the mighty completed structure. Later, he would not be able to recall a single "problem" in reconstructing the towers. There were challenges, but nothing that even rose to the level of what he would consider a set-back or failure. He consciously struck the very idea of *problems* from his vocabulary.

'*Challenges*' were exciting and meant to be overcome with positive energy. This was Tony's language. He knew what he had to do, had full confidence in himself and in his team, and their focus was united and intense.

Riggers on Base Tower A - Photo Ted Bryan estate

In contrast, in the matters of his heart, his focus was not so perfectly beamed on the details. He was certain of his love for his new fiancé, but the early doubts were never completely buried. Early in the relationship with Mara, there were tiny warning fissures that all was not as solid as it seemed. Yet, he did not examine those tiny cracks. As an engineer, surely he knew at some level that no structure flawed from the beginning could withstand the ravages and stresses of time. He hoped for the best, something alien to the engineer's creed: engineers don't *hope*, they *make* it happen. In retrospect, he wished he'd paid closer attention to the warning cracks in the veneer of the new relationship.

Now, he peered at one of the critical components of the connector piece. He examined the steel plate that had buckled and collapsed, contributing to Tower A's tumble. He had measured the corresponding plate on Towers B and C. In both those towers, the plate was about an eighth-inch thicker. Those towers had withstood the hurricane's wallop at their midsection. Tower A with the slightly thinner plate had not. An eighth of an inch and a tower had fallen! Such a small difference in construction, with such a devastating result. Little things mattered; little areas of weakness had a way of becoming massive chasms under stress.

While Ted wanted everything rebuilt exactly as it had been before, Tony suggested the coupling plate for Tower A be made a little thicker, as it was on the tower that had remained standing. Ted agreed, and in the end, that was the one modification engineered on the rebuild.

At the beginning of the rebuild, Tony brought the shop crew photos of the towers as they had looked right after the hurricane. Then he showed them old photos of the intact original towers.

"This is our goal," he told them, holding up a picture of the intact towers, "We want them to look and perform exactly the way they did before Hugo."

Tony wanted the factory workers to have a sense of the whole picture so he never tired of bringing them updates and photographs of the ongoing project. He knew it was important in instilling a sense of pride in the technicians for them to understand how the fasteners and bolts or braces they were manufacturing would fit into the final product.

"I wanted them to know how important every single part was in our success," he told me, "I mean can you imagine spending all your time manufacturing just one specific part and never getting to see how important that part was in the completed tower? I always tried to involve them in the entire process so they would feel the same sense of accomplishment I felt when it was all done."

He would bring them photos of the project as it progressed -- pictures of the mangled towers, the crumpled steel carted away, the remaining tower base now cleared of debris and awaiting it's new upper half. And as the engineers and technicians began to assemble the new shiny steel pieces, they paid close attention to matching the measurements exactly with the remaining tower base.

"If we were off, even by a little, it wasn't going to fit," Tony explained, "It had to be perfect."

Ted Bryan concurred, noting that bolts off by as little as 1/16th of an inch would need to be re-engineered.

As the parts were fabricated, Tony was busy with a multitude of other tasks. To perfectly recreate the geometry of the tower, he had to measure every slope and make detailed notes and measurements. Every part of the remaining towers had to be analyzed for structural integrity. STADD, the computer program used for that purpose, helped him analyze joint loads, stresses on each beam and connection. A careful geometry analysis was needed to be sure all the parts would fit together exactly. He conducted a complete, meticulous, visual analysis of any corrosion or thinning areas of paint that might indicate compromised structure over all three towers.

Perhaps the single most critical piece in the entire rebuild was the connector square. This 17'x 17'x 30' piece was the link between the standing base, and the newly rebuilt upper section. The connector square was to be manufactured completely at the Columbia factory. Tony made multiple visits between Columbia and Charlotte, remeasuring and analyzing. The connector square took shape, under Tony's precise and careful instructions.

Ted Bryan continued to be faithfully present at the tower site every day of the many months that the towers were being rebuilt. Ted had overseen a few other tower rebuilds, but nothing with the scale and complexity of this project. His excitement mounted as he watched his towers slowly transform. What a tedious and complicated process! No wonder other firms had refused to touch this job!

Each day Ted carefully recorded the day's progress in the station log book. He would meticulously list what the builders accomplished in his neat handwriting, then date it, and close the book with satisfaction. Even on the days when rain and wind prevented any tower work, he faithfully recorded the delay. On those days when rain threatened, but it was uncertain if the crew would be able to work, Ted stood on the loading dock of the transmitter building looking out over the field. The hawk, waiting at his post atop Tower B would exchange glances with him. Ted's phone rang. No, they weren't coming today. Ted sighed and returned inside the building to record the log entry: "Rain imminent. No tower work today."

He watched with growing respect and awe as the steps towards success were slowly checked off. He was there more than anyone else, except for perhaps, the hawk. He gazed upon his towers with just as much piercing intensity as the scowling raptor. The hawk that had watched Tony when he first arrived to view the crippled tower, returned to his perch high atop Tower B, day after day. When Tony or the riggers climbed Tower B for measurements or to conduct their structural tests, the hawk would occasionally screech and with a great flap of wings, glide above them, floating on thermals in wide circles. When they lowered themselves slowly back to the ground, the hawk would settle again on a beam, and tuck his wings tightly against his sides. High above them, he watched with dark, unblinking eyes. Ted also watched carefully, impressed by the care with which Tony oversaw the project. When the work ended for the day, he smoothed the paper in the log book, and wrote, "Stacked two sections, 9 and 8 on C tower. 9/15/90."

The tower construction crew was hired by Kline to carry out the actual tower rebuild work. They were responsible for cutting down the old metal, helping Tony assess the structural integrity of the intact portions, and then reconstructing the towers piece by piece.

Construction Crew - courtesy Ted Bryan Estate

It was a family business. The foreman was the father, his three sons the tower erectors, and his wife responsible for the books. As soon as the chief engineer at Kline had asked Tony if he wanted to assess the job, Tony requested this particular tower crew. He'd worked with them before and trusted them. He knew the foreman would certainly not cut corners or take chances when it was his own family that would pay dearly for his mistakes.

While Ted and the tower crew were always at the field, Tony travelled back and forth from Columbia, working between the shop and the tower field. He was in continual contact with the foreman, often driving to Charlotte in the morning, then back to Columbia in the evening.

Sometimes, after the crew finished for the night, Ted remained behind. He watched the lengthening shadows of his towers stretch across the field. As his gaze slowly climbed the wounded half tower, he cringed slightly at the desecration wrought by the hurricane.

"Soon," he whispered, as the night descended, and the last rays of the sun soothed the beheaded antenna.

Tower C, the first one to be rebuilt was slowly taking shape. While the workers were methodically stacking each rebuilt section on C, the painters were scraping the old paint from Tower B. Once the paint was removed, the workers ascended the tower with buckets of paint and huge spongy mitts on their hands. They started at the top, and dipped their mitts into the paint then smeared it on the tower. It took 50 gallons of paint for each tower! The portions of A and C that were reconstructed on the ground were spray painted, but the parts of the tower that were still standing had to be painted with the mitts while the workers dangled high in the air with the paint buckets nearby.

The tower upper section was almost a mirror image of the bottom with the rectangular section between the two tapered portions. Tony knew the key element that required particularly special attention was the rectangular connector piece. Everything hinged on how well that piece brought together the old intact section with the reconstructed top section. While Tony was confident he could build the connector piece, it was the one unknown of the whole operation. The bottom half of the tower, still intact, would be carefully measured and analyzed. Back at the shop, the top section and connector piece would be constructed. The top section would be assembled and even fitted on the connector piece at the plant. They would know the top section would fit exactly to the rectangular section. What they would not know was if the connector piece would fit exactly on the base, and they wouldn't know that till they lowered it onto the tower bottom at the field. If it didn't fit, it would be Tony's responsibility to take it back to the shop, reconfigure, and fix any mismatch. That would translate to wasted time and money. Tony would do everything in his power to insure the match was perfect the first time.

CHAPTER EIGHT
A Towering Hope

Assured that he had found his perfect match, Tony married Mara. Any subconscious reservations were shoved aside. He had grown up in a large and loving family, with parents who loved each other and remained together until his father died of prostate cancer. He had always known that one day, he wanted to marry, and when he did, he wanted to "do it once, do it right, and do it forever." When he asked Mara to marry him, he was committed to emulating the love and faithfulness he had seen in his own parents.

Consistent with his optimistic personality, Tony rarely saw the bad in people. He gave people the benefit of the doubt, trusted in their goodness, and believed and hoped that what he put into relationships is what he would reap. He never questioned that he might struggle in marriage. He had seen a strong marriage growing up, and he loved family. He was excited to start his own.

This woman that he married had had a tragic life -- a husband killed in a plane crash, and then the struggle to raise her son alone. Not only did Tony fall in love with Mara, but he came to love the son as well. Skylar was only eight years old when Tony married Mara, and he legally adopted Skylar.

Skylar was the ideal son for an engineer. He was constantly taking things apart and then putting them back together to see how they worked, just as his new father had done as a child. When Tony worked on the construction of the Lake Murray dam spill gates, just a few miles from his home in Columbia, Skylar accompanied him, helping to hold the tape measure and record the measurements.

Tony bought a beautiful home with a view of Lake Murray. He and Skylar worked together, side by side, engineering and then building a koi pond. They carefully placed each piece of shale in an artistic curve to outline the koi pond, which they could see from their deck as they sat together sipping lemonade. When Skylar grew up, it was no surprise that he too became an engineer.

Tony settled into married life. Kline was as close to perfect as any company for which he could hope to work. With the WBT-AM tower rebuild, he was making a name for himself in the tower industry. He had a beautiful home, lovely wife, loyal son, and glorious profession. The murmurs of disquiet were easy to smother at first. Optimism and the conviction that he could do anything he put his mind to had served him well in his youth, in college, in his career, and now surely in marriage.

A year after marrying, Tony and Mara had a baby girl. They aptly named her Starr. She really did become the star that Tony's world circled. Increasingly, Tony noticed tremors of struggle in the marriage, but he continued to suppress concern about the early ripples of discord. He loved his son, and the new baby girl completely captured his heart. A peace-maker at core, and anxious to avoid struggle and conflict, Tony tried as best he could to smooth the rough patches that snagged the tranquility of the marriage.

Tony never felt Mara quite understood his passion for towers, but he had enough enthusiasm for both of them. She did to some degree understand the danger, and it concerned her. Given the circumstances that had taken her first husband from her, it was not surprising that she feared for Tony on the towers.

"Don't go too high up!" she would plead, as he left on yet another trip to the tower.

"I won't," he would say, kissing her goodbye, and holding little Starr snugly against his chest, then gripping his son's shoulder. But he would. He had to go up high. He could not get enough of the sky and the view of the trees and cars so far below him, like a tiny toy village. How could he not climb to the top of the world? Knowing it frightened his wife, he didn't tell her. He promised her he would not go up too high, but he had to, and so he did.

Perhaps it was because of her first husband's death in a plane crash, but Tony's wife did not love to travel. While they vacationed as a family at times, she increasingly resisted travelling to Tony's relatives. Tony struggled to comply with her desire, though his own heart yearned to see his beloved family up north, and his extended family in Spain. He longed for his children to know their Spanish relatives and embrace their heritage. Most disturbing was his wife's reluctance to gather with his family in the United States. He had visited frequently with them his entire life. Two of his sisters had even lived with him when he was first working for Kline. They had been inseparable as children, and maintained that close relationship as young adults. He reluctantly complied with her requests to curtail visits. His unhappiness with the situation grew, but he didn't want to endure the conflict that resistance caused.

As his children grew, he longed to bring them overseas to the beautiful country filled with relatives he had visited nearly every summer of his life. However, he stifled the desire as best he could, not understanding why this piece of himself was a threat to the woman he loved. Bewildered, and saddened by the separation from his extended family, Tony wanted to please his wife, and he would do nothing to hamper the marriage or jeopardize his relationship with the children. So he acquiesced, and let this portion of his life founder.

Resentment smoldered, but he suppressed it. He repeated his mantra that marriage should be "done once, done right, and done forever." His wife had her reasons, and while he didn't necessarily agree with them, he would respect them.

However, his heart was breaking with the sacrifice. His family, angry and hurt, curtailed contact with Tony. They sent cards on his birthday with brief cursory notes. The gulf widened, and Tony suffered, but was determined to save his marriage.

Not all was pain at that time. Skylar soaked up his father's instruction in understanding how and why things were built. As little Starr grew older, she shared her father's love of photography, but the engineering aspect of his life was less compelling to her.

"None of that was really my cup of tea," recalled the daughter Starr, as a young adult, "I loved old things, really old things. Like I love all the old buildings in Europe...and I love Spain. But how things work...not so much. I am the kind of person that if something is broken, I want it fixed. I don't necessarily want to be the one to do that or understand how it is done. But whenever Dad would walk in a building, he would look up, and notice how it was constructed. And he would want to tell me, using all these technical terms that I didn't understand. He knew how everything was made. But he was always patient, and would try to make me understand.

"For example, there is a street in Charleston that has a huge bump in it. And every year, they repair it, and level it, and every year, the bump comes back. I remember asking Dad, 'Why does that bump keep coming back!?' And he explained that there is a pipe under the street. Because of the way the soil is in Charleston, the dirt settles but the pipe is fixed and doesn't settle -- so the bump keeps returning as the land settles around the pipe. No matter what I asked him, he always knew the answer."

"Always try to understand the principle," he would tell Starr, when she grew frustrated, not understanding the technical explanations he offered.

"If you understand the principle, you can make sense of anything," he said.

Starr remembered that admonition, one of a constant stream of 'slogans' that her father was so endearingly filled with. To this day, if she is struggling to understand something, his words come to her: "Try to understand the principle of the thing."

Unfortunately, what Tony himself could not quite understand was the principle of why so much of what he loved was slowly being eradicated from his life. To him, the principle of marriage was mutual respect, support, and appreciation. When that is gone, he noted sadly, the marriage is over. The marriage was becoming a problem without a clear solution. All the blueprints for marriage that he had been raised with did not seem to fit this particular disintegrating structure.

The already rare visits with his New York and Spanish family became fewer and fewer. Mara became increasingly concerned with his time spent working, frustrated with broken engagements, and angry with Tony being late because of the frequent, unavoidable conflicts at work.

Starr heard her mother's more vocal expressions of anger, and saw her father retreat into deeper silence and somewhat bewildered hurt. She knew at one level that the marriage was crumbling, though could not recall anyone specifically ever telling her that.

She is quick to point out that she loves both her parents, and that she adores her mother. She does not blame one more than the other, though doesn't quite understand how such a level of disagreement could arise.

"My mother is not a bad person. She had a lot of tragedy in her life, and she overcame a lot. I really admire her for that. She is not perfect, but who is? She has always been a great mom. I understand the way she reacts, though I guess I react more like my dad."

Starr hates conflict, and like her father, would prefer to acquiesce rather than ruffle feathers. She is like her father in other ways, too.

"Mom eats like a bird," Starr told me, "But Dad and me, we love to eat!"

Tony travelled a great deal, but when he was home, he catered to his beloved Starr. Starr danced ballet her entire life. Whenever he was home, Tony was the one that took her to practices. When she had roles in the productions, which she often did, Tony would go to each practice and volunteer backstage. Every year, Starr was selected for a role in The Nutcracker. One year when Starr was only six or seven years old, one of the dancers for the ballroom scene called in sick just thirty minutes before the show.

"Tony!" cried the producer, "We need you! Can you put on this tuxedo and do the ballroom scene?"

Tony looked up from his work on the set.

"What?! You want me to do the scene?"

"You've seen it a thousand times!" begged the director, "and the tux looks to be your size. We have half an hour. I can show you what to do."

Tony put on the tuxedo and practiced the ballet scene for half an hour, and then when the curtain opened, he was in his first professional ballet. Not only was he an exemplary tower builder, but apparently he was not a half bad ballet dancer in a pinch. His perennial optimism and can-do attitude could be equally applied to balancing on a beam 2,000 feet in the air, or conquering a 'plie' and 'grand jete' on the ground.

CHAPTER NINE
A Towering Perspective

There are many similarities between the work of tower builders and fighter pilots, though few WWII aces moonlighted as professional ballet dancers like Tony had. Having their work site thousands of feet above the earth was one of the more obvious commonalities. However, I hoped to find a connection that might help explain what the WWII beacon was doing at the tower site. To that end, I returned to the Atterbury-Bakalar museum in Columbus, prowling for helpful WWII veterans. After the pilot John spoke with me, several other WWII pilots who volunteered as docents at the museum offered their opinion regarding the WBT-AM beacon.

James Peters Sr., a relative spring chicken at 88-years old was eager to talk about his experiences. Jim had been a B17 flight engineer and ball turret gunner. His missions had flown out of Italy, and his targets had largely been crucial oil refineries. He concurred that navigation during the war was limited, by today's standards.

In fact, he noted that of 13,000 B17s in the US, over half were wiped out in training practices alone. A major source of accidents was poor navigation skill and inaccurate equipment, particularly in inclement weather. I waited breathlessly for him to say, "If only we had had aircraft beacons like the one at WBT-AM," but unfortunately, he did not. He could not imagine why the beacon was there other than to mark the towers.

Next, I called Adolph Scolavino, a flight engineer from the list the museum docent sent me. A woman answered. Adolph was in his 90s, still living with his first wife, both in good health. She checked my credentials, and then told Adolph there was a writer who wanted to ask him some questions. She was clearly the gate keeper.

Adolph was born June 16, 1920, in Providence, Rhode Island. He had joined the military in 1939. His dream was to fly, and he would do whatever it took to learn to pilot an airplane.

"I wanted to fly! I loved airplanes. When I was a kid, during the depression, I scrimped and saved till I raised $2. For $2 you could go to the airfield and a pilot would take you up for half an hour in a little biplane."

Back then, $2 was a lot of money. His money could well have been useful for food or clothing, but the young Adolph wanted to fly, and fly he would. He became a flight engineer on a B17, and was based in Panama. While there, he took private flying lessons. And then the war came, and he was sent to the Kunming base in China. His first heavy bomber mission was to target the Linsi Mines near Beijing. The Linsi Mines had some of the finest iron ore in the world, used by the Japanese for guns and ammunition. He encountered plenty of heavy flak, but came back unscathed from his first three missions. On his 4th mission, he flew over Rangoon. It was a night mission, and his plane was shot down. The crew bailed out, and parachuted down into the dark jungle, not knowing whether they were in enemy territory or not.

"We all had cuts and bruises, but we survived. Fortunately, we had bailed out on the British side of the Burma jungle. Some Gurkha soldiers found us. Do you know what they are?"

I quickly googled Gurkhas. The Gurkhas were from Nepal, but fought in the British army. They were fierce fighters. One commander once famously said, "If a man says he is not afraid of dying, he is either lying or a Gurkha."

"Well the Gurkhas brought me and my crew to the British encampment," continued Adolph, "A young doctor patched me up, stitched me together. Did a fine job of it too. I asked him where he had been trained as a doctor. He told me he wasn't a doctor; he was just a bloody lands corpsman! Anyway, the Gurkha was looking very longingly at my medical kit in my backpack. So I gave it to him to thank him for saving me. He was so elated, he took out his Gurkha knife and gave it to me. I still have it."

"You told me you were shot down on a night mission. How did you navigate at night?" I asked hopefully.

"Oh we used a compass," he said, "It wasn't too hard. You just know where you take off from, keep the aircraft on the correct compass line and time how fast you are going so you know when you have gone far enough.

"Now coming home was another matter if you happened to get lost. Then you come in on a radio beam. Do you know what that is?"

"Indeed I do!"

"Well you would beam in on a radio station. Sometimes we would get a Rangoon station. You had to try to beam in on the base radio beacon. If you were riding on the beam, you would hear beep, beep, beeeeeeeeeep. If you got outside the beacon, that would just be a faint dying out beep. You stayed on the beam by listening for the sound."

"What kept the enemy from sending up radio beams to confuse you?"

"They did do that," agreed Adolph, "The Germans would send up the beam and if they were closer, their beam would be more powerful than the Scotland base beam. So the pilots would follow the beam, find themselves lost over the Atlantic, and run out of gas. You are right. That did happen. The most famous 'radio' flying story was the *Lady Be Good* story. *Lady Be Good* was a B24 that landed in the desert, by accident, flying on a beam. She went on a bombing mission, and on the way back, in the dark, picked up a radio beacon beam. She flew right past the beacon, and didn't know it! She was still flying on the beam...but going away from the base! She kept flying and by the time the pilot realized his mistake, she ran out of gas. They landed in the desert, in the middle of the Sahara. They all died. They didn't find the plane till around 1970 when an oil survey crew found it. It shows the inaccuracy of radio flying."

It also shows that if a light beacon had marked the spot where the base was, the pilot might still be alive. I tucked that tidbit in my beacon theory box.

WBT Beacon -- courtesy WBT Radio

CHAPTER TEN
A Towering Risk

Unlike dancing a ballet which may be nerve wracking but relatively safe, tower erecting is considered the most dangerous job in the nation. Not once, in the months of interviewing Tony had he mentioned he was in any danger. He repeatedly insisted that as long as he stayed focused, he would be safe. It was only when I began researching what was involved in the tower erecting industry that I realized Tony may have downplayed the risk.

"In the old days, there were very few safety measures," Tony said, "Now OSHA standards require a full body harness which hooks onto a cable. If you fall, you only fall about two inches and the bracket catches. Older towers don't have that cable system. So like on the WBT-AM towers, you would attach lanyards to the section you are climbing, then hook your safety vest to it, climb a little, reattach the lanyard higher, and make your way up the tower that way."

Even a cursory look at the websites devoted to tower erecting reveals one deadly incident after another. Tower erectors are described as having the single most dangerous job in the nation.

An OSHA study from 2008 showed that tower erectors chance of dying on the job was more likely than in any other profession -- more than soldiers, more than coal mine workers, more than aircraft pilots. Tony insists that there is a difference in the mortality rates and accidents of the cellular vs broadcast tower industry, though the published mortality rates of the two are usually lumped together. He is very protective of his own broadcast industry, and wishes that the statistics reflected the difference in safety maintenance. He asserts that the broadcast tower workers tend to be older, more experienced, and very concerned with safety regulations. He suggests that it has different challenges that perhaps make safety a greater issue. As always, Tony was hesitant to disparage anyone or anything

Nonetheless, the OSHA Comparative information from that 2008 article certainly suggests that people who want to live long lives should weigh risk vs. benefit when entering the tower erecting profession. In the article, the authors note that "Tie on Or Die" is synonymous with safety in the tower world, yet many tower workers ignore this.

Why had Tony not mentioned this aspect of his industry? The National Association of Tower Erectors (NATE) publications indicate that industry dangers cannot be overemphasized. NATE writers claim that with the explosion of the cellular market, there is a huge need and drive to erect cellular towers quickly. Unlike some dramatic YouTube videos made to show the exciting moments of tower building, true tower erecting is slow, tedious work…or *should* be. Therein lies the problem.

Safety on a tower relies on careful adherence to the safety precautions. When rushing to meet a deadline or becoming complacent with safety equipment, the rate of death or injury skyrockets. While there is not a large number of deaths overall, considering the small number of tower erectors, it is a disproportionately hazardous occupation.

Surprisingly, in the heyday of radio and TV tower erection, when safety precautions were even less, there seems to have been fewer deadly occurrences. Some NATE commentators suspect the profit driven explosion of the cellular market puts burdens on tower workers to proceed at a pace that is not likely to lead to collecting retirement benefits.

A recent YouTube video was removed following an outcry by OSHA. In that video, a tower erector climbing a thousand-foot tower only tethered himself when he paused to rest. All other times in the video, he was "free climbing," and claimed OSHA rules allowed for that practice which "is wide spread." The YouTube commentator claimed that most tower erectors free climb, as to spend the time hooking on to the tower per safety regulations would be too tiring and time-consuming.

Tony however claims that there is no OSHA allowance for free climbing. It is dangerous, and it is prohibited. As the video climber indicated, that is not to say that some of the very experienced or the very incautious do not do it on occasion. However, nothing in OSHA standards allows for the practice.

Tower Workers on WBT-AM Blaw
Knox, securely tied on to the gin pole -
courtesy Ted Bryan estate

What kind of safety measures were employed, or at least, were *supposed* to be employed? Tower erector safety manuals have pages and pages of precautions and describe elaborate devices designed to keep the tower

109

worker alive. The NATE safety manual is replete with requirements for Personal Fall Arrest Systems, full body harness, decelerations lanyards, anchorages, D rings, ropes, straps, webbing, lifelines, two-step safety locks, shackles, clevis, carabineers, hooks and connecting hardware with the tensile strength of 5,000 pounds. With all these precautions, how could anyone die?

The major cause of death for tower workers is not following the safety procedures, not taking the time to hook on at each appropriate time and place. Tony, in climbing the older Blaw Knox tower, would have used the old fashioned and more tedious lanyard system. Had he been careful to snap on the lanyard every painful foot upward that he rose? No wonder Mara had been so frightened as he headed off to work.

However, Tony explained, "I've been doing this a long time, and I really don't think of it as dangerous. I mean, you always need to be careful, and be aware, and be focused, of course."

Amazingly, Tony was never afraid, and never had been.

"I never really worry when I climb. I started my career on the tall towers, 1,000-2,000-foot towers, and I never think of it as dangerous. This is pretty simple, but it is true...an engineer once told me, 'When accidents happen, it's usually when someone loses focus on what they're doing.' There is a dangerous element to it, but as long as you stay focused and pay attention, you will be ok.

"In the old days, you really did hear less about accidents. I think the short tower explosion [cellular tower boom] led to a whole lot of young and inexperienced workers. Then there were more accidents but I think they were maybe not as aware... you know, didn't have the experience and took some precautions for granted. For example, before they 'tied on', they may think, 'oh, I can reach over there while holding on with one hand before I go tie up a little higher.' They might get a little too confident, not attach 100% before hooking off the old section. Initially, with the cell market boom, people wanted to do things more quickly, more economically. Then accidents happened."

Tony notes that in any new, growing industry, there is an adjustment period. As the cellular industry expands, he is confident there is a greater awareness and adherence to safety measures which will continue to improve as the industry grows.

"The heavy tower industry, the big towers, back in the old days had more experienced guys working. They just didn't take the chances that it seems younger, new guys take. Then the short tower guys started jumping into the heavy tower business, and well, you can't lose focus or be overconfident on a tower."

When initially pressed to talk about some of the accidents or dangers he had experienced himself, Tony was uncharacteristically reticent. He never liked discussing negatives -- not in his work, nor in relationships, nor in his past. He was a very optimistic man, and usually had to be cajoled into admitting any difficulties he had encountered along the way.

Despite the dangers, Tony never questioned his career choice. He had not known initially that he would work on towers. All he knew was he would be a civil engineer like his Dad.

"I knew I wanted to work in steel construction of some sort," he said, "But when Kline hired me, they had openings in the Tower engineering department, so that's where they sent me."

Tony hitched his future to towers, and never untied. He always knew how to protect himself from the falls that made his profession so daunting. "Tie on or die!" If only all his tethers in life could have remained so trustworthy, so secure.

CHAPTER ELEVEN
A Towering Connection
Fall 1990

Tony glanced at the beacon as he climbed, but he was not nearly as enthralled with why it was there as I was. In fact, he didn't give it a moment's thought. He was busy paying attention and "tying on." Tony and three other tower riggers had scaled the middle WBT-AM tower. Tony, with the least experience of all of them on an AM tower, had learned the hard way about being particularly careful not to *miss* when hopping onto the tower. While the tower was not as electrified as normal, the moment when his foot touched the ground ever so slightly was one he would not soon forget.

Good morning! Better than a cup of coffee, that little jolt early in the morning! The connector piece would be arriving soon. For now, the riggers were busy inspecting the middle tower. They had come to greatly respect and admire Tony. He had not had a great deal of experience on AM towers, but he was competent, and respectful, and always eager to learn and to help wherever it was needed. His reconstruction of the tower pieces seemed nothing short of miraculous to them, though the critical connector piece they would be installing later today would be the most crucial test of his skill.

They uniformly liked him. And he was fearless. Nothing seemed to perturb him. This made him an exceptionally pleasurable target. Now as they climbed, the three brothers winked at each other. They had a surprise for their courageous friend.

Tony, as always, was focused. He climbed steadily, carefully hooking the lanyard every few feet. At one point, he rested, about two thirds of the way up. The first third of the climb had been along the outside of one face, from the tapered point near the ceramic base and angling out till he reached the self standing vertical section. At this point, he climbed straight up, and the face was about 17 feet across. As he began scaling the top third of the tower, it angled in again towards the tapered top. The width of the face narrowed as he climbed, the slight movement or deflection of the tower more noticeable as he moved closer to the tapered thin tip.

Deflection, or movement, is critical in all tall structures. Engineers design for deflection. If tall structures could not gently sway from the force of the wind, they might snap. There were wind load standards built into every tower based on the expected wind of the area. The ability to measure wind load accurately is much better with computer modeling nowadays. In the old days, prior to the computer technology, engineers "over-engineered", or built structures with higher wind-load capacity to compensate for their imprecise ability to accurately measure. Tony explained that the code today may be more stringent than the code of the past in what a structure could withstand, but the old WBT-AM towers still met code because of the strong construction from that pre-WWII era.

It was very peaceful on the tower. The tower was in the middle of a huge field in a relatively rural section of the city. It was increasingly quiet as he climbed, just the sound of the wind and the ever present birds drifting in the clouds. He could hear traffic below, but it was muffled. He thought with a sudden spasm of joy that he was in a beautiful place, looking out on a view so few people on earth would ever be privileged to see. The insight gripped him but a moment, and then he remembered the caution his father, his professors, and his mentors at Kline has so deeply instilled in him: *Pay Attention! Focus!*

He was focusing on his work, inspecting the metal beams as he climbed, and didn't notice the other riggers winking, and slowly moving their bodies in unison.

By the time he had reached the pinnacle, a mere 19 inches across, the riggers were more vigorously swaying. The thin fishing pole like top of the tower accentuated the movement, and suddenly Tony found himself swinging through the air. He clutched the tower. It was perhaps only a few inches of deflection but it felt like a whole lot more than that, coming so unexpectedly. The riggers had carefully noted that Tony was properly tied on and secure before they began their little prank.

Tony good-naturedly laughed, clinging to the tower and shaking his head at his co-workers.

"OK," he said, "That got my attention. You better watch your back now!" he warned.

*****

While the work was proceeding on Towers A and C, Bob White explored the cost of "greasing" the guy wires. Bob knew the corrosive effects on the guy wires would eventually weaken them, and by the simple act of keeping a coat of lubricant on them, the superior construction would last as long as the towers. Lubing guy wires is not as simple as it may sound. Tower B was a working tower -- continuing to transmit throughout the period of the rebuild. As Tony had explained, it was "hot" -- that is the radio frequency (RF) surging through the antennae was powerful enough to burn anyone unfortunate enough to touch it either when ungrounded, or at "hot spots" like the insulators. The insulators are all along the guy wires to reduce interference with the signal and to insulate the tower from the ground. Thus anyone greasing the cables had to be very careful not to contact the insulators (using his body to connect the two halves of the insulator.)

Bob contacted various companies who could do the work and the lowest quote was $70,000. Having worked on towers since the 1970's, Bob knew he could tackle the job himself at a lower rate. He called a close friend, Bret, who had worked on similar jobs many times with Bob, and the two of them undertook greasing the guy wires themselves. While Tony's work rebuilding the structures was proceeding calmly and without mishap, Bob was not quite so fortunate.

In order to grease the guy wires, Bret would slowly ascend the guy wire itself, greasing as he moved up the wire. He was hanging below the guy cable during this procedure, which took two hours per wire. A rigging system was devised with two safety measures to complete the task and reduce the risks. One rope was attached at the tower, just below where the guy wire was anchored. That cable would pull him slowly up the guy, with Bob below adjusting the tension from the free end. A second rope attached Bret to a safety line that looped over a pulley system near the top of the tower vertical section. This safety line allowed Bob, operating a hoist from the ground to literally pick Bret up in the air and lift him past the dangerous insulators. This procedure was accompanied by Bret detaching the safety line from below the insulator, and reattaching above it, just below the next set of insulators. Once Bret had greased one of the four guys, he would move the safety line pulley and load line pulley to the next leg of the tower, and Bob would 'belay' while Bret rappelled back to the ground so he could ascend and grease the next guy wire. The hoist with an electric motor took the brunt of Bret's weight, but Bob would hang on to the rope to adjust the tension needed to keep the rope properly taut.

This procedure can be fraught with difficulty. In fact, Bob had known of a family of tower workers using the same sort of pulley apparatus that ended in tragedy. The tower riggers were a man, his son, and the son's best friend. The wife operated the winch, or hoist that would keep the proper tension on the cable.

Apparently, they had incorrectly wound the rope onto the equipment called a "cathead hoist." The wife was holding onto the rope from below as the winch was raising her family from the ground. When the winch operates as it should, the person holding on to the rope

117

does not need a great deal of strength to keep the proper tension on the rope.

As the wife watched, applying the correct tension from below, something snagged the workers riding up the tower, causing the winch to be yanked sideways allowing the rope to unwind. Suddenly, the small woman was the only force left to hang on to the quickly descending weight of her husband, son, and friend. The rope snaked through her hands, cutting her skin and muscle to the bone. She had no chance of hanging on, and her family and friend crashed 1,000 feet to the ground. All the men were killed instantly on impact.

But back to Bob and Brett. Having successfully finished greasing one guy wire, and repositioning the pulley for the safety line, Bret signaled to Bob that he was preparing to rappel to the ground. As Bob watched, Bret unhooked his safety belt from the tower. Just as he started putting weight on the rope, the pulley came loose from the strap tying it to the tower. It came tumbling down as Bob watched in horror. Bret somehow, in a maneuver nothing short of miraculous, not only managed to catch a hold of the tower to keep from falling, but caught the pulley as well.

Bob later reported that this was, "Between you and me, an act of God," but also fortuitous in that Bret didn't have to reclimb the tower with the pulley. It had only fallen about ten feet. He clambered back up, reattached the pulley, securely this time, and moved on to grease the second guy without incident.

*****

Massive Crane ready to raise
connector piece - courtesy Ted
Bryan estate

Tony considered what he could do to repay his tower
rigger friends for the stunt atop Tower B. He had little
time to plot. Having finished his inspection on the
tower, he noticed the large flat bed truck pulling into
the field, the connector piece firmly lashed down. He

119

glanced at Tower A, and visually compared the space where the connector would be placed with the connector piece itself. Revenge on his tower erecting buddies was forgotten.

"It looks good," he thought. He was confident his measurements had been correct. He had pored over his drawings and calculations countless times. At the shop, the entire top of the tower had been reconstructed and assembled. He knew that from the connector piece up, the tower would be perfect. But the connector piece had to fit. That was the one unknown of the entire process. Would it fit?

"Of course it will," he thought, slowly climbing down while the other riggers laughed and joked with each other above him, "It has to."

He thought of his conversation with Mara the night before. She had talked about her day, what Skylar had done in school. She hadn't asked a lot about the tower. He had told her it was an important day coming up, but he didn't explain in much detail. She didn't seem very interested in the details, though she had told him she hoped it went well, and especially that he be careful and safe.

When he reached the last ten feet climbing down, remembering the wake-up jolt that morning from touching his foot to the ground, he jumped off the tower. Ted Bryan, as usual was there. He was filled

Preparing to hoist connector piece -
courtesy Ted Bryan estate

with anticipation. At last, his tower was to receive the first invaluable piece of its resurrection.

"It looks good," said Ted, pointing to the flat bed truck with the connector piece.

"Now we'll see if you get what you paid for," said Tony.

Ted smiled at him, "I have full confidence we will."

Ted wasn't feeling worried or antsy, only very excited. If there was a problem, he knew Tony would have to fix it. He knew the only one that was likely feeling a little anxious was Tony. Frankly, Ted could not believe how smoothly the process had proceeded thus far. The most minuscule miscalculation in any portion of the connector piece would render it useless. It had to be perfect.

They heard a screech and looked up. The hawk had settled back on his lookout perch on Tower B. He peered at the connector piece, and then back at Tony.

The construction foreman sauntered over to Tony. He told him the crane was in place and all was ready. Workers were already cutting off the straps that held the connector piece in place. The tower riggers were coming down off Tower B.

The crane had arrived on the back of a huge truck. Its giant arm had to be assembled on the field. Because it was close to two hundred feet long when fully extended, the crane was backed against the fence, the arm assembled, and then raised. The crane was then slowly driven across the field with the unwieldy arm a top-heavy behemoth. Bob White held his breath as it jostled over the uneven patches of the field. Ted winced as it teetered slightly over one particularly bad bump. If the crane went over, there would be more than broken towers to worry about. However, the crane made it safely to the area near the tower, and it was finally time to hoist the connector piece. The operator raised the crane arm and swiveled it to connect to the 17'x 30'-foot connector piece.

Tony stood next to the foreman. They watched as the crane operator and workman attached the bolts that would secure the connector piece. The foreman's sons had already climbed to the top of the base of Tower A. They were in position, ready to wrestle the connector piece into place.

"This better work," said the foreman to Tony.

"It better," agreed Tony.

"How's your heart rate?" asked the foreman, as the crane slowly lifted the connector piece.

"Like I just finished a triathlon," laughed Tony

When the piece hovered just above the tower riggers, before they touched it, they had to equalize the radio frequency (RF) of the base to the dangling piece. Otherwise, the strength of the RF would burn them. For this purpose, they had what looked like giant alligator clips, similar to what is used in battery cables for cars. First the rigger clamped one end of the clip to the tower. As the connector piece was maneuvered within reach, the rigger clamped the other giant clip on a beam. A huge orange plume arced in the air, and as always, the riggers cheered the spectacular fiery display. With the piece now safely equalized to the RF of the tower, they grabbed it and with the help of the crane operator, faces red and muscles straining, manhandled it into position. They motioned to the operator to slowly lower the piece.

Lowering Connector Piece - courtesy Ted Bryan
estate

Connector fits perfectly - courtesy Ted
Bryan estate

Tony had one hand over his eyebrows, shading his eyes from the sun, still low in the sky. He was not exactly praying, but he was intent, willing the four corners to match. He knew they would match....they had to match. He was confident they would match. But if they didn't...

They will.

Approximately 200 bolts would be tightened to secure the connector piece to the base. The workers slowly tugged the giant steel square to the pivots -- the corner lugs. As the crane winched the piece down, it settled exactly, perfectly into position.

Tony sighed deeply and watched as the tower workers began to thread and tighten the bolts. There were about 50 bolts on each face. Tony watched as one by one, each bolt slowly dropped precisely into place. He could hear the sound of the metal being turned against metal.

"It's looking good," said Ted, approaching him.

"Only about 195 bolts to go," said Tony.

Throughout the morning, the workers high atop the tower labored. Section by section, they tightened each bolt. Every bolt dropped into position, and one by one, the carefully engineered posts bound the tower to the critical connector piece. It was late afternoon when the final bolt was ratcheted down, and the tower worker pumped his fist in the air.

Tony glanced at the foreman, with a grin. Ted smiled and nodded at Tony.

"Perfect," Ted said, "I really don't know how you did it, but it is perfect."

Tony exhaled, and swiped a hand across his brow.

"We know the rest fits," he said simply, "The only piece we had to worry about was the connection between the two parts. As long as the connection is perfect, the whole thing will be perfect."

CHAPTER TWELVE
A Towering Pain

When had they lost that critical connection? Had they never had it? How had all his hopes and dreams come to this? What had happened to *do it once, do it right, and do it forever*? Tony knew his world was about to topple.

For a while following the WBT-AM rebuild, all seemed well, at least on the surface. Every Sunday morning, Tony and Starr would go to church. Mara and Skylar had no interest, and rarely went with them. However, Starr remembered those Sundays with great fondness. They would attend the service at 'Our Lady of the Lake', and then go out to eat.

"That's why I went," laughed Starr, "I loved to eat!"

After their lunch together, they would go to the golf course driving range, and smack golf balls. Tony recalls that Starr showed promise as a golfer. Starr no longer plays golf at all. For her, the golf was fine, and church was bearable, but the lunches were glorious.

Starr was catered to by both parents, the little princess adored by an older brother, and the priceless beacon of Tony's life. The years marched on. Skylar left for college, and the arguments between the parents grew louder and more frequent.

Simultaneously, ominous changes were occurring at Kline. A large corporation bought out Kline's tower division and Tony stayed with the tower division. The first acquisition worked out well. Then there was a second acquisition. There were adjustments, and not necessarily good ones, in Tony's opinion. With characteristic determination to make the best of his situation, Tony remained with the new company and worked as hard as ever. He tried to look at the good that remained in his work, and tried to forget the growing struggles at home.

He convinced Mara that they needed counseling. He could no longer ignore the persistent fears and concerns. They went to one counselor, but when she complained that she didn't like him, they tried a second. Again, according to Tony, she was unhappy with what the counselor was suggesting, and she refused to go to any more sessions. Meanwhile, Kline went through a third acquisition, and Tony knew he needed to consider a new course of action. This was no longer the company that he had known. With despair, he was coming to the same conclusion about his marriage. Finally, there was no recourse, and the couple separated.

Now, Tony sat across from his daughter at his tiny kitchen table. The one bedroom apartment was not nearly as spacious as the home he had left. If he sat in his living room, he could look in one direction and see the entire kitchen. If he looked in the other direction, he could see his bedroom. The entire apartment was smaller than one room of the home he had owned with his soon to be ex-wife.

Starr was looking around the apartment. She was newly a teenager, and would dutifully follow the court orders that she spend one weekend with her mother, and the next with her father. She never tried to fight what was happening to her. She was a child. She loved her mother, though she wished, like all kids that her mother were more patient. She loved her father, though she wished perhaps he didn't have to be gone so often working. It never occurred to her to try to fix the marriage, or urge her parents to reconcile. She had a rare ability to compartmentalize her love for each. As an adult, she would not recall ever thinking that it was something that she should or could try to change.

She was a compassionate and observant child. She knew her father had grown increasingly quiet in the months leading up to the move to this apartment. He had always been gentle and kind to her. That didn't change in the slightest. But she would catch him with a distracted, sad look on his face at times. At first, she assumed it was troubles with Kline. At age 13, she knew very little about what he did. She knew that whatever it was, it was time consuming. She knew he worked on towers, but she really couldn't visualize what that entailed.

He travelled many weekends, and sometimes she would not see him for several weekdays either. When he did come home, he would bounce into the house like a golden retriever puppy, full of stories and excited, infectious joy. He always presented her with a small gift of some sort. But Starr noticed increased steely silences from her mother when he returned; subtle hurts drifted in the air like noxious fumes.

As time went on, the exuberance of Tony's returns subsided. Instead, he seemed troubled. He didn't speak as effortlessly about the wonderful work he was doing for Kline. There was hesitancy in his talk about his work. He never showed outward anger, never raised his voice. But Starr knew something was off kilter. She heard some discussions between her parents. She gradually cobbled together an understanding that Kline was not what it had been. It was changing in ways that her father was finding increasingly difficult to cope with. He became more withdrawn and even quieter. The tension between her parents escalated. Starr might not have been able to describe what she observed as a marriage tottering, but she could feel that there was a growing strain between the two people she loved most in the world.

The absences her father's work necessitated were the way her world had always been. She thought it was the way it always would be. She accepted it without analyzing whether it was what should be, or what she wanted. Nonetheless, it was impossible not to overhear her mother's concern.

She knew as the difficult year progressed that her mother was unhappy and increasingly critical of the toll Tony's hours took on their time as a family. However, she also saw the wounded silence of her father, the incomprehension that something he loved, strived to do his best at, could be denigrated.

Kline continued to change in ways Starr didn't understand, but saw her father's growing unvoiced despair. The rift in the marriage expanded; the anger and hurt of both parents spiraling downward in lock step. Finally the dissolution of the life she had always known could no longer be avoided. The rift was complete; the connection irrevocably severed.

Starr does not recall ever being sat down and told her parents were breaking up. She knew that was where the fights were headed. She claims that the break-up did not disturb her, though she doesn't understand how anyone could disagree enough to cause a divorce. Nothing seemed worth that level of discord to her, but she also admits she might not understand, not ever having married. So while her parents never specifically explained why they would no longer be all together, Tony sadly told her that he would have to move out. They would both love her, and she would never lose either of them. But things would be different now. By court order, Starr would see her Dad every other weekend and certain days of the week, and certain holidays.

She hated the court restrictions. She hated going to the apartment. It was not her home, and it was not where her friends and her possessions were. She hated that whether she felt like it or not, she would be with her Dad on the court appointed days. It was not that she didn't love him and want to be with him; it was that she was given no choice in the matter. Her life was completely out of her control now, and while she could accept her parents' divorcing, she could not easily accept the consequences to her freedom.

The morning before he moved to the apartment, Tony made his daughter breakfast like he did every morning. Breakfast was never fancy, but it was always Tony that made her breakfast. Sometimes it was "fake churros." Starr had had the real thing in Spain, and with some derision, called the grocery store variety "fake," but they were frequently served and "were not bad."

The morning Tony left, melancholy saturated his normally buoyant spirit. If there was any way he could be there giving Starr "fake churros" the following day, he would have been. There was no way. He could no longer pretend the fracture could be repaired. For the divorce to proceed by South Carolina law, the couple must be separated a year in separate residences. Besides that, he had stayed much longer than he should have, far beyond the point of any real hope. As he handed Starr a plate of "fake churros," he thought, "How can I give her up?" He looked at her with her dark curly hair cascading around her beloved face, her eyes somber and unreadable.

Things had long ago reached the point where he could no longer tolerate the sham of a marriage. Nonetheless, he had tried to rebuild it, if not for the sake of the marriage, for the sake of his love for Starr. But like any good engineer, he saw that if a structure required two legs to remain upright, one alone would never stand. The marriage crumbled completely, and Tony knew he could not resurrect it from the shattered pieces that were left. He was an engineer, not God.

On one weekend, shortly after Tony had moved into his small apartment, he made breakfast as he always had for his beloved daughter. It was "his" weekend with her. He had felt a great relief when he had first settled into the tiny place. He felt for the first time in many years that he was free to breathe, to be the person he had stifled for so many years. But how he missed those morning breakfasts and evening prayers with his girl!

Starr took a plate of eggs from her father, and looked around her. She had never kicked or screamed or even complained during the separation of her parents. She had been an observer, not quite understanding, not letting herself be consumed in the vortex of grief. She was only a child, and perhaps not quite able to verbalize that this was not what she wanted, but aware that was true nonetheless.

"Why am I here?"she asked quietly.

Tony sat down heavily across from her. His eyes were dark pools of limitless grief.

"I don't want to be here," said Starr.

I have lost her, thought Tony. I have lost everything. What could he do? He understood that for him to argue, or to insist would be futile. It was her *mother*, after all. He would not satisfy any desire to lash out at the mother if it meant the child would suffer.

"I want to go home," said Starr.

The marriage was dead, and for all intents and purposes, Kline as Tony remembered it was dead as well. The second acquisition by a competing company transformed his beloved Kline into something he no longer recognized. Each acquisition moved Kline further from the tower traditions that had so distinguished them. And now, was his daughter to be lost to him as well? That day was perhaps the lowest point of Tony's life. He returned Starr to the home where he had once harbored so many dreams and hopes. Little was said to her mother, other than right now, Starr needed to be home.

Tony returned to his empty apartment, and sat down in the living room. He looked in one direction and saw the kitchen, and in the other direction, the bedroom. His whole world now was not much bigger than his arms could reach. The man who just a day ago had stood fearlessly on a thin beam of steel 2,000 feet in the air with the earth stretching to the horizon all around him, sat in the tiny empty apartment that was for now his world.

Tony by Richmond Tower - photo by Vicky Kaseorg

CHAPTER THIRTEEN
A Towering Solution

A whole new world opened to pilots when radio air to ground communications began. Could the WBT-AM towers have done something of value during the war besides broadcast radio shows before radar and modern navigation equipment were available to airplanes? I was certain they had, albeit based on little more than romantic hopefulness.

In 1926, radio stations began their role in the lives of pilots, with the new communication technology. Shortly thereafter, teletype stations could transmit weather conditions to pilots, and finally, pilots began to use radio stations to pinpoint their position.

John the pilot had described the use of what was known as four-course radio range. Four towers that marked the four corners of a square would transmit the letters A or N in morse code. The pilot could discern which beam he was flying on, and which quadrant he had entered depending on whether the morse code of the specific letter grew louder or fainter as he flew. Where the beams intersected, a steady hum would come over the radio, and the pilot knew he was on the correct path.

In 1933, 90 stations with a lighted tower and rotating beacon were in place as part of an airmail pathway.

They spanned an 18,000-mile route, with the stations about 200 miles apart. The beacons flashed in a specific rate to indicate what kind of landing field was nearby -- 24 to 30 flashes per minute for beacons marking airports, landmarks, and points on Federal airways, 30 to 45 per minute for beacons marking heliports.

The Department of Commerce established an east coast 763-mile pathway of such beacons in the 20s and 30s to aid airmail pilots! That pathway from New York to Atlanta was called the Contract Air Mail Route or CAM-19. I found partial maps of the beacon placements. There was one in Greensboro, NC, but I couldn't find a map of the beacon path that included the Charlotte area.

The reason for the beacons gave an interesting insight into the history of the mail service. Airmail pilots took seriously the famous postal slogan, "Neither snow nor rain nor heat nor gloom of night stays these couriers from the swift completion of their appointed rounds." The transmitter/beacon system was set up so that pilots could deliver mail overnight, and fly in conditions when visual navigation was impossible. They would do whatever it took to complete their appointed rounds.

There was a period of time during the Great Depression, when FDR took over the private mail carrier contracts and gave them to the Army. The mail was delivered in reconfigured bomb hatches of AAF planes. Had the army installed beacons?

I wrote to an assortment of web-masters of the historical aviation sites who had posted information on the air route. I even wrote to the Smithsonian, but was sobered by their disclaimer that they received thousands of requests for information and my query might never be answered. Rest assured, they still appreciated that I took the time to write to them, and would I consider a tax exempt donation?

My search finally uncovered an old air route map. One of the stops along the way was indeed Charlotte. The old Cam 19 route was: New York, NY--Philadelphia, PA--Baltimore, MD--Washington, DC--Richmond, VA--Greensboro, NC--*Charlotte, NC*--Spartanburg, SC--Greenville, SC--Atlanta, GA-- in 1929 (contracted to Pitcairn Aviation) -- a total of 803 miles.

While Charlotte being a stop along the route didn't yet prove the WBT-AM towers had been one of the navigational beacon stations, the transmitter building *had* been erected in 1929, when the route was established.

Scott Fybush, who writes a "Tower of the Week" column, had visited the WBT-AM site and claimed in his column that the chief engineer had shown him a "searchlight" that sat atop the transmitter building, added during WWII. He said snipers were positioned on the roof as well, fearing attack to the station.

I was certain Ted, the retired WBT-AM engineer, had told me eight years ago when I first met him that it was a rotating red beacon, not a searchlight. But, if it *was* a searchlight, with snipers ready to obliterate saboteurs, then like the Cincinnati tower, WBT-AM must have been broadcasting something that bothered the enemy. On the other hand, if it was a searchlight, it wasn't a red beacon guiding the airmail planes, a sexier role.

The WBT-AM historian believed the beacon on the transmitter building was a searchlight. I argued that a searchlight would be white, not red.

Undeterred, the historian felt it was used to guard the station against snipers during WWII. He surmised that the station was an enemy target. During that time, there was great fear about what the Nazis might do. They had bombed oil tankers right off the North Carolina shore. He claimed many cities went into blackout mode at night as a result of that fear. This intrigued me since blackout conditions would be daunting to pilots, unless they had beacons on the ground to navigate by.

An online beacon expert, John Eney, promised to help me find the location of the beacons on the airmail route. He claimed Charlotte was not on the route, but *was* a major hub for one of the first and most prominent airlines, Eastern. Eastern travelled along the early airmail route, and beacons certainly lit the path from the 1929-1939 time period.

While John was busy hunting beacon locations in his historic documents, I perused the World Wide Web for clues. The internet is filled with interesting 'chat rooms', including one group discussing WBT-AM. They were clearly a knowledgeable crew -- some had even owned radio stations.

One writer discussed a Raleigh radio station, and contributed a fascinating nugget of information: "*Funny you would mention WPTF. One of my old bosses of many moons ago was employed there, and he once talked of a 'request by Uncle Sam' that the nighttime pattern be directed toward the Southeast so as to be used as a navigation aid by ships and airplanes!"* (Radio Discussion Board)

WPTF, out of Raleigh, North Carolina, was asked by the United States government to transmit specifically as a navigation aid to both ships and airplanes. Since WBT-AM was always the powerhouse AM station of the southeast, the government *may very well* have made a similar request of them. I wrote to the army, the airforce, the Smithsonian, and the Civil Air Patrol. None of them could find any evidence of any military use of WBT-AM, nor any clue as to who had installed the beacon or why.

As I was despairing of making any sense of all this, John Eney had explored the Airport Directories from 1929 until the 1940s. No mention was made of beacons on the lighted airways system at WBT-AM until 1937.

The 1937 Airport Directory listed WBT-AM as the only Charlotte station strong enough to be used by aircraft as a direction finder source. The directory also described the presence of the red rotating beacon. John believed it was entirely possible the beacon was to notify pilots of the station locale when they were using the station's signal to navigate. This ADF or Automatic Direction Finder system can still be used today for pilots to fly using radio signals to navigate. Since this was the first mention of the beacon in the historic documents, it appeared likely that 1937 was the year the beacon was installed.

Initially, John Eney didn't feel Charlotte was part of the airmail route, as none of his sources confirmed that. I insisted I had found documentation it was on the route, though felt a little sheepish arguing with an expert. He wrote back a short time later, having found a map that showed Charlotte was indeed on the Federal Lighted Airways system.

Now my search was two-fold. Was the beacon an airmail beacon or was it used in war navigation?

It had been a radio station transmitting Christmas music in Pearl Harbor that had guided the Japanese to their bombing target that dragged us into WWII. How fitting it would be if the WBT-AM signal had assisted Allied pilots to navigate to safety with the beacon's guiding light to mark the station.

On the other hand, very few airmail beacons remained. Such a role for the WBT-AM beacon would be equally exciting. Either way, I was certain I was on the verge of discovery. Little did I know the "verge" would take an entire year.

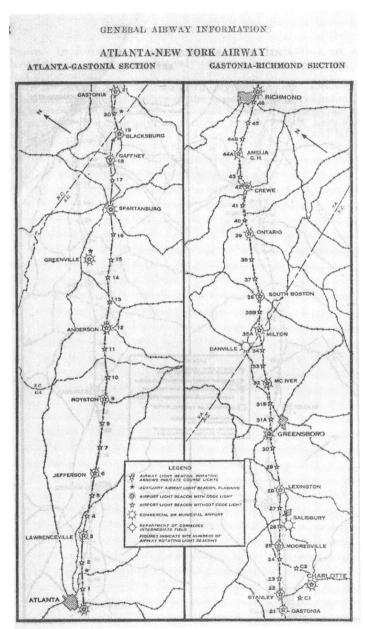

Map of Federal Airway System showing Charlotte spur on CAM 19
Dept. of commerce 1937

CHAPTER FOURTEEN
A Towering Adjustment

Starr was glad the long bitter war years between her parents were over. She doesn't recall feeling sad or sorry for herself that her parents were no longer together. However, she hated being in the middle of their expectations, the beacon in both their worlds. She hated that both parents wanted time with her, and she could not cut herself in two. She didn't exactly feel that they pressured her, but she felt the pressure nonetheless. She hated the court orders that decided when she could be with her Dad. She hated her mother's concern that time spent with Tony might indicate Starr loved her less. She did not want to abide by the court's dictates, but she had no choice.

"Why couldn't I just see them whenever I wanted!?" Even fifteen years later, I detected anger, not at her parents, but at the inflexibility of the schedule it imposed upon her.

She had always been very close to Tony, but with the divorce, if he was out of town on her visitation day, she did not get to see him. Tony could probably have tried to alter the visitation days, but it would have prompted more struggle, more fights...and he had had enough of fighting. He wanted desperately to see his beloved daughter, but he also wanted to be sure she never felt herself to be a pawn in the turmoil with Mara. He tried never to show disrespect for his ex-wife, even when he felt his plans with Starr were sabotaged. Starr was aggravated at being caught in the middle, but she never rebelled in any obvious way. She received good grades, never got in trouble, never acted out. She occasionally gave her parents a hard time, but in general, Tony recalls her as being an exceptionally good kid. Starr was also quick to point out that she owed her success and who she became to both parents.

"My mom is a wonderful Mom," she said firmly, "And I owe everything to her. I love her and I admire her. She is not the bad guy." Tony looked respectfully at his daughter, and did not object to the statement. In fact, he agreed, "I always believed she was a good mom."

"Just yesterday," Starr recounted, "Mom and I went to the Nutcracker together. I danced the Nutcracker almost every year growing up, so it was really special to go there with her. My mom had so much she had to deal with in her life. Given her background, I think she has done really well."

However, Starr agrees that in the years before the divorce, Tony saw less of Starr than he wanted, and she felt a little tossed about by circumstances beyond her control. She acceded that her mother did not want her traveling to Spain, or even to Tony's stateside family. It was a frustration to Starr, who loved her relatives, but again, as a minor, she could not impose her desires on the circumstances. Tony desperately wanted to take her to Spain, but he bided his time.

When the divorce was final, and Starr was fifteen-years old, he began to travel with her as he had always hoped one day he would. A whole new world opened to them, and their mutual love of exploring new places, visiting with her Spanish and northern relatives, and eating new food (especially that!) was finally satisfied.

They both reveled in the Spanish lifestyle. All day long, they walked. They walked to a little restaurant for lunch, and then walked to another place for coffee, and later another place for desert. They wandered the village streets, noticing the old architecture, the beauty and slower pace of Spanish life. Sometimes they would still be wandering long after the sun set. Everyone is always outdoors in Spain, Starr told me, and log many miles walking.

Tony, knowing Starr's love of historic buildings and cities took her to all the surrounding villages and regions as well. They discovered a little street called "Calle de Fonseca." Together they explored their namesake street, assuming some long ago relative had first lived there. Starr now says she could not imagine settling down, and not traveling. She claims, "It is my dad's fault. He is the one that made me love wandering to new places."

Starr also remembers his constant explanations of why and how things worked, and she recalls asking him about the things they saw together in Europe. Tony was beaming as Starr recounted her memories of asking him to explain things to her. He had not realized that she had valued that aspect of his engineering character, and it warmed his heart.

·

"What are those, Dad?" Starr recalls asking him, on one trip to Spain.

"Solar panels, and wind turbines," he explained.

"How do they work?"

Tony excitedly explained in technical terms, and when Starr cocked her head with a perplexed look on her face, he launched into a discourse on "the principle of the thing."

Their close relationship was becoming even more special. When Tony travelled, he called Starr almost every night. He was steadily rebuilding, and even strengthening the relationship he had once feared could never be resurrected. Starr took a photography class in college, following in her father's footsteps of a love affair with the camera. She hoped to get a new, fancy camera for Christmas.

"Do you know how to use one?" I asked her.

"No," she conceded, "But Dad will teach me."

She showed me several photographs she had taken, and then Tony pulled out a framed shot he had snapped from the top of Mount Wilson in California. It had won first place in a photography contest.

However, he nodded at Starr and said, "She's really talented, isn't she?"

"I'm not as good as Dad," she said, ducking under the overflowing adulation.

Meanwhile, as the two continued cementing the strong bond that had been forged early on, Tony finally left the corporation that had acquired Kline. He found contract work that allowed him to work out of his home. He would not leave Columbia and lose any possible opportunity he could snatch to see Starr. He did much the same work that he had done for Kline, and continued to build his reputation. The tower world is relatively small and the major players are known by the other established engineers in the field. Tony continued to work the only way he knew how -- with all his heart and soul. As his reputation for excellence, innovation, and creative courage grew, his personal horizons continued to expand. He was traveling frequently with Starr and reestablishing the relationship with the family he had sorely missed during his married years.

He tried to exercise each day with characteristic persistence. Tony had been a swimmer in both high school and college, good enough to be on the Citadel swim team. He now was running and biking regularly as well, and entering triathlons. He sometimes won first place in his age group, often placing in the top three. Trophies lined his dining room counter. He bought a carbon fiber racing bicycle, and developed his racing skill with the same determination and excellence in which he approached his engineer work.

When the divorce was final, Tony had his beautiful home on the lake back, and his former wife settled in a beach home they had purchased. He recognized that his house was far too large for a single person, but he liked the fact that when Starr came home from college, she could sleep in the same bedroom in which she had grown up. And in the morning, when he wasn't traveling, he could sit on the back deck, and look out over the lake, the very lake for which he had helped create the dam spill gates so long ago with his son, Skylar.

Unlike Starr, Skylar was unable to avoid taking sides in the divorce. For five years, Skylar didn't speak to Tony. It clearly was a painful memory as Tony mentioned this and he did not elaborate. They did eventually reconcile, and see each other now, but not as often as Tony wishes they could. I remembered the koi pond he had shown me that he had built with Skylar, now choked and overgrown with weeds.

"It was really beautiful when we built it," he recalled, as we stood on the deck looking down at the pond, "You should have seen it then."

During the time that Tony was contracting with the Seattle firm remotely, a tower company headquartered in Canada approached him. Would Tony consider joining Turris, not as an employee, but as a partner?

"Heck yes!" said Tony, "I mean how often is someone offered part ownership in a successful company!? I jumped at the chance." They formed a U.S. corporation called Turris Engineering Inc.

Tony loved Turris and his work with them from the beginning. He remembered what made him love Kline so much, and tried to replicate that special relationship between management and employees. He loved being in control of his schedule, profits, and work load. There was no comparison between being an employee, and being an owner in a company like Turris. He had always hated the "office politics" that inevitably sprung up while working for other companies. He had been so distraught watching helplessly as Kline Towers transformed to something he no longer felt a connection too. Now he was in control of his destiny, at last. He got to call the shots. He was firmly regaining all he had lost.

When asked if he ever despaired during those difficult years, or felt like giving up, he didn't pause in shaking his head and answering firmly, "No! Whenever things got bad, I would remember my Mom's words She always told me, 'If you think you have it bad, go knock on someone else's door.' I was taught that there is always someone out there that has it worse. When my Dad was fighting cancer, Mom used to bring Dad to the cancer center where he would see people younger than him, fighting cancers much worse than his."

She helped Tony's Dad and Tony not to focus on their problems and struggles, but on what they had.
Tony's mother taught him to count his blessings, and to build with whatever materials he was handed. Perhaps she, even more than her engineer husband, was the one to give Tony the courage and strength to rebuild after the storms that topple towers and marriages.

"If you're walking and talking, you have nothing to complain about," she told him. It was a lesson he clearly absorbed. And from the first tower he ever climbed, Tony never stopped thinking, "I am the luckiest man alive."

*****

"That first tower I climbed... I was thinking, 'Get me off here!'" said Bruce.

Bruce is a construction manager and has worked on towers all over the world since 1992. He works on cell towers, which Tony often intimated is a very different business than that of broadcast towers. The first tower Bruce climbed was "only a 60-foot monopole." I asked him if he had any other thoughts, feelings, or emotions as he scaled that first tower.

"No," he said, "Just *get me off of this*!"

When asked what type of person would enter this field, Bruce said immediately, "Crazy!"

When Bruce started climbing towers, he echoed Tony that OSHA had few safety restrictions.

"Back in the old days, we just climbed with a belt and butt strap."

"Butt strap...is that what they are officially called?"

"Well no...I think they are called Klein straps."

"What are they for?"

"Well, we would free climb and when we needed to rest, we would tie off and rest hanging on the butt strap."

"You free climbed?"

"All the time. Still do."

"Does OSHA allow that?"

"Mmmm...well....no. But it is actually safer than tying off every step. I would much rather free climb than follow the OSHA regulations." Later, other tower climbers I met reiterated that same theme – free climbing was so time consuming that most workers believed it was safer than following the OSHA regulations.

"Isn't that more dangerous? What if you slip?" I asked.

"Then you are dead. But every tower climber knows you don't let go with one hand till you are hanging on with the other hand."

"I would think so!"

"If you have to tie off every step, you get really tired. And it takes forever."

"Have you ever had any close calls?"

"I've had a few heart checks," he said, "But I never fell. A friend did though."

"What happened to him?"

"He died. He fell 800 feet."

"Was he free climbing?"

"Yes."

"Did that make you nervous about the next time you were on a tower?"

"I'm always a little nervous. Once you think you're invincible, it's time to get off the tower. Every time I go up, I am aware of the danger."

When I talked with Tony about Bruce's experiences, he cautioned me to remember that the cellular tower business was a somewhat different setting than the broadcast tower world. Tony reiterated that in his business working on broadcast towers, the safety regulations were followed. He felt that accidents occurred much less frequently than in the cellular field. He claimed that in general, the workers on broadcast towers had been in the business a long time, had years of training and experience, and were very cognizant of the need to follow OSHA requirements.

Bruce's experience seemed to be very different, and supported Tony's view that the cellular business was a different beast altogether. Bruce's first time up a tower was not a particularly pleasant experience. The tower was behind a thrift store in a trash littered industrial area. A liquor store was nearby. There was no beautiful view from the top, even if he hadn't been consumed with wondering what he was doing there in the first place.

The second tower he climbed was a 175-foot antenna on the outskirts of Denver, Colorado. That time, he was not yet an official tower worker. His job was to deliver supplies to the tower site.

"But I wanted to go up...see what it was all about. It was really beautiful. You could see for miles. I tied off at the top and just sat down and looked around. That climb was what sparked the desire to work on towers." It always struck me as a little incongruent for swashbuckling tower climbers to lyrically describe their appreciation of the beauty from atop a tower.

On one job in Wyoming, Bruce had scaled a 400-foot tower on an antennae farm. The towers were to be dissembled. He was removing the beacons from the very top of the tower when a commotion below caught his attention. One of the workers had placed a hot torch on a pile of plywood. The plywood burst into flame and within seconds, Bruce watched with horror as the fire, whipped by winds and fueled by extensive underbrush in tinder dry conditions, spread with terrifying speed. Within seconds, the anchor points for the guy wires were surrounded by giant hot flames. Bruce called his girlfriend from the cell phone he had tucked in his pocket. He wasn't sure if he would live. He knew the guy wires and anchor points could become so hot as to buckle and disintegrate. If that happened, the tower was coming down, with Bruce clinging to the top like a marshmallow slipping off the stick into the campfire.

He knew he didn't have enough time to climb down safely. Instead, he remained atop the tower the whole time.

After the first few moments, the fire had consumed the brush around the tower and was now raging across the flat pasture. The anchor points held and Bruce was safe. While he watched from his advantageous perch, the fire roared towards distant homes. Bruce alerted the TV stations and firemen, and provided updates and photos from his phone. He stayed on the top of the tower for 2 1/2 hours while the fire consumed 15,000 acres. He watched the firemen swiftly etch fire breaks in the distant field, which successfully saved the homes.

Over the years of working on towers, he had seen many accidents and knew of many deaths. Yet, he didn't feel the tragedies were so much due to not following safety regulations as to the unreasonable expectations of those who needed the towers. Bruce had a very different attitude and take on the issues of safety and concerns with the cellular industry than Tony did. Tony had a good relationship with the vendors in the cellular industry, and as always, adhered to a safe and responsible methodology. Bruce had a less charitable outlook.

"I lay the blame on the customers and turf vendors," Bruce said angrily. The customers are the cellular companies and the turf vendors are the middle men, the ones who hire the contractors who will build the towers. The cellular companies want the towers built as quickly as possible and put the squeeze on the turf vendors to find contractors who will build the fastest. It doesn't matter to them, Bruce reported, that the pace at which the workers would have to erect the towers would lead to unsafe practices, and careless construction.

"What happens if you just tell them that time frame is unrealistic?" I asked.

"They find someone else," he said, "If you want the job, you have to do it as fast as they want it done."

Bruce was very open about his opinion that it was impossible to follow OSHA regulations, and still remain in business. And worse, Bruce contended there was always a glut of "illegal aliens" willing to work at the breakneck speed for lower wages. He felt it made the climate even more cut throat, more dangerous, and less profitable.

Certainly, dangers abounded in this business. He mentioned that he had never been on a tower during a bad storm, and didn't know if one would be electrocuted if lightning struck.

"I don't want to find out," he said. He always got off the tower when storms approached.

"How did you know when to get down?" I asked.

"We could feel it in the tower, before you could hear the thunder or see the lightning. It's like a buzz in the tower...like you feel the electricity in the air. You get off the tower when you feel that." This is oddly comforting, that the tower itself warned its builders of danger.

Bruce felt that despite the growing list of OSHA safety regulations, there were less accidents when he first started in the business. And to add to the incongruity of that, he reported that drug use, at least in his experience, was rampant among tower workers in the "old days."

"You mean...right before they climbed the tower?" I asked, incredulous. I was truly flabbergasted. Tony, in stark contrast would never have condoned such dangerous or foolish activity. Tony, aghast, told me he had never experienced anything remotely like that in his career tower building.

Bruce continued, "Yeh...we would go in the support building, do a few lines [of cocaine] and then climb the towers. Maybe that's why we were never too scared up there....Drug use was common back then. I don't do it now, of course."

Using mind altering drugs and then dangling a thousand feet in the air seemed less than the epitome of wisdom, but at least the tower workers in the United States wore a belt and "butt strap" so they could tie off to rest. Bruce told me that when working on a tower for the Sultan in Brunei, an Indonesian Island, the Malaysian tower workers would climb with no safety equipment at all.

Tony was shocked when told what Bruce had said about drugs. He was wondering in fact if Bruce had been telling a tall tale. Never would Tony have compromised safety, integrity, or wisdom in such a way. His voice was outraged as he listened to my recounting of what I had been told by Bruce.

"WHAT? I have never heard or seen anything like that in my work. I mean...drugs before going up the towers? That is crazy! I know of lots of workers who will have some beers when they are done with work...never, ever before!"

When I had first contacted Bruce, our interview was postponed as he had just gotten out of the hospital.

"A heart scare," he told me, "but I will be fine. Just have to make a few life changes."

He added that he doesn't climb the towers much anymore, "I'm older, not as agile and nimble as I used to be. But the stories I could tell you!"

CHAPTER FIFTEEN
A Towering Danger

While Tony was reticent to focus on any of the negatives of his work, like Bruce, he had witnessed many dangers and tragedies. It was not surprising that Tony didn't wish to discuss any unpleasant parts of his work, or his life. He was a man who clearly did not dwell on negatives or failures. His positive attitude had won him his first job, his success at The Citadel, his success rebuilding the Blaw Knox towers, and now part-ownership of his own prestigious tower company. He did not see the point in recounting struggles or disasters. Under protest, he agreed to share a few stories of this type.

"The most tragic incident was when I had to go to a site and inspect it, right after a man was killed there," he recounted with a heavy sigh. "It was a tower in Georgia. After the main structure is installed, the various components are put on. This particular tower had an elevator system. The person involved was responsible for putting the elevator cables in the structure and connecting them. Sometimes people don't do what they should do."

He paused, clearly not enjoying this memory.

"The worker wanted to get down to a lower level quickly, so instead of climbing down and doing it the slower, safe way, he decided to slide down the cable. You know how a fireman slides down a pole? That's what he did on the cable. The cable was not connected, and it overhauled itself and went down on top of him."

Tony explained that even when the cable is not yet connected, there is an end that can support weight, and there is an end that cannot. It was unclear if the man thought the cable was connected, or thought he was grabbing the safe end and grabbed the wrong one. Either way about it, he crashed down and the cables piled on top of him.

Tony's job was to inspect the site and determine if it was safe. If possible, he would ascertain what had caused the accident.

"I could still see the blood down there. It was very sad. He either thought he was on the connected end...or he just wasn't thinking. That is why people have accidents," he said, "They lose focus in life."

Being single minded and attentive is hard to maintain for very long. That quality appeared to be one of Tony's strengths. Tony had often mentioned the need to always pay attention, and never lose focus on the job.

"Multi-tasking is a myth," said Tony, "I mean it. Did a little research on it. You may think you are multi-tasking and doing several things well, but in reality, you are doing several things poorly and no faster than if you just focused and did one at a time."

Suddenly, I heard some squealing, and then I heard him yell, "Hey! I was just about to pull in there....Sorry Vicky, I am pulling in to fill up with gas and this guy cut right in front of me!" I smiled thinking how ironic this was in light of what we were discussing.

"So where was I? Oh yeh, multi-tasking. So look it up. You can't do two things at once well.

"Anyway, my job was to inspect and survey, and determine what was damaged. It was really hard to see the blood there. The foreman started crying. Big burly iron worker. A grown man crying! That was really hard to watch. Sometimes these guys work together for years. They are like family to each other. It was hard."

Despite seeing such a horrible accident, it did not deter Tony from continuing to climb the towers.

"Over the years I'd heard of other incidents and I was able to cope with it. I knew how important it was to pay attention and not lose focus and I would be ok. I just didn't really think of the dangers.

"I gotta tell you though; I just got back from a job on a tower on top of a tall building. Just being up there with a 360-degree view of the city, it was breathtaking. I mean, I had to be out there at 1 a.m. because that is when the tower wasn't being used, and I couldn't wait! How many guys can't wait to get out to their job at 1 a.m.? I love what I do. I can't wait to go to work. This is corny, but I like to say, 'I get high on being high.'"

Tony's passion for his work was boundless, as was his enthusiasm. How did he deal with the inevitable struggles and obstacles that all jobs entail, especially one with so much potential for mishap?

"By praying," he said immediately, "and just persevering. Never give up. When I was at The Citadel, I had my school work, the military responsibilities, a tough major, and then coupled with that, I was on the swim team. It was a huge challenge to do all that. But I just focused and kept a positive attitude. Keeping a positive perspective is really critical in succeeding."

Tony was continually racing from one job to another, and our interview sessions were often caught in spurts between flights. Did this tireless man ever have down time or pursue leisure activities?

"Yes," he exclaimed, "I thought I told you. I race in triathlons. [*A nice relaxing pastime*] In fact, I gotta go in a couple of minutes -- it is time for my training run. I don't have many daylight hours left."

*****

Tony had another heart wrenching tower experience that involved an apparatus called a gin pole. The gin pole is a rigid structure with a pulley or block and tackle system on the free end such that it can raise or lower parts and equipment above the section of the tower being worked on. The fixed end is attached to the tower. The free end is above the tower, and can be used like a crane, but one that is attached to the tower and can move up higher as needed. Since towers can be two thousand feet high, obviously no fixed ground crane could be used to raise heavy equipment or build the upper sections. For those situations, a gin pole is used.

The gin pole in this particular story was 160-feet long, a ten-ton behemoth being used on a 2,000-foot tower. 'Jumping off the gin pole' is when the riggers remove the assistive lifting device from the tower when the work is completed. The most dangerous part of tower work is almost always when equipment is raised or lowered.

Tony and the tower crew were removing the gin pole in one piece, having finished installing the final top equipment on the 2,000-foot antenna. The people below them were dots from that dizzying height, the flatbed trucks smaller than sugar cubes. The work on the tower top was done, and it was time to 'jump off the gin pole' and call it a day. Tony was securely "tied on" as always, and was doing his job, paying attention, and not thinking about the fact that a whole multitude of things could go wrong, making gravity his mortal enemy.

The crew attached the massive gin pole to the load line, which was carefully pulled away from the tower by the tag line so the heavy piece would not crash into the tower. Tony watched as the gin pole was slowly being lowered down the tower, and was now right alongside him approximately 1800 feet in the air. At that moment, the hoist suddenly stopped, and the massive gin pole lurched. The movement of that ten-ton piece of unwieldy steel set the top of the 2000-foot antenna swaying. Tony clung to the tower, feeling himself swinging on the noticeably moving tower spire. It was probably a good thing he had eaten only a light lunch.

"Will the tower stand?" he thought, "Is this the end?" Again, through no fault of his own, it looked like he might be free-falling without a parachute the length of six football fields to the oh-so-distant ground. It was one of the few times that Tony admitted to being terribly scared. Slowly, the gin pole quieted, the tower stopped swaying, and Tony exhaled before climbing down to terra firma.

*****

When I first met him face to face, I was to spend the day watching him work on a tower. I drove to within feet of the tower, and could see it on the other side of a barbed wire fence, but must have missed the opening to the field. I called Tony's cell phone.

"I can see the tower. But I can't figure out how to get there," I moaned.

"I'll be right there," he said, after I described where I was. I certainly could have found my way if he had just given me directions. Instead, he left the work site and drove out the quarter-mile to find me, and lead me to the tower. When he found my car, he hopped out of his SUV, and came to where I was parked. He stuck out his hand and clasped my own as though I were a dear friend. We had spoken over the phone many times over several months, but had not met face to face until that very moment. His handshake was as firm and confident as the man himself.

"It is a pleasure finally meeting you," I said, meaning it. This was a man of genuine, kind, pleasant nature. I had known I would like him from the many phone interviews we had already conducted. I was not surprised to see him bend over backwards to be polite and helpful in making the field day profitable for me. Tony's demeanor and bearing exuded warmth and respect, with an aura of competence and intellect. He reminded me of his description of his father.

The construction manager at the Richmond site, Hunter, owned his own business and often worked with Tony. Both travelled all over the United States to erect

Rigger during WBT-AM rebuild dangling on
section supported by Gin Pole - courtesy Ted
Bryan estate

towers. Hunter had been erecting towers since he was
16 years old, and had worked on some of the largest
antennas in the world. When I was standing at the base
of even the relatively small 400-foot tower and looked

163

up, the height was impressive. I asked Hunter if he was ever afraid.

"There was only one time where my life was really in danger, and you bet I was afraid then."

Hunter had been setting a second piece on the base of a tower. He was eighty feet in the air, and had signaled to the crane operator to slowly lower the piece onto the stub or connection point. He had just put in the stub, which is basically a pivot point. The crane operator misunderstood the instructions to lower the piece, and instead picked the whole piece up, with Hunter dangling from it, eighty feet above the ground.

Hunter clung to the beam as it swung through the air, the ground swirling beneath him. He heard the shouts of his brother but could not speak himself with the dizzying motion of the dangling piece of metal.

Hunter's brother, working nearby on the base, hurtled himself to the edge of the tower. He managed to grab the piece, precariously keeping his own balance. Muscles bulging and aching, he wrestled it back from the abyss, forcing the stub into position. Hunter slid off the stub onto the tower base, and grasped his brother gratefully.

"I could've died," said Hunter, "But that was the only time I remember being scared."

I spent that day watching the tower erectors on a 400-foot tower in Richmond. Their job was to reinforce the tower based on Tony's recommendations following his "Feasibility Structural Analysis."

Whenever new equipment is added to a tower, it puts new stresses on the tower. The conscientious tower owners have regular stress analysis conducted to be sure the tower is strong enough to withstand the new stress. Tony was often responsible for conducting the analysis, and if necessary and feasible, reinforcing the tower.

This particular tower was part of the Richmond "Smart Zone Emergency System" that had been put in place in the late 1990s and was fully operational in 2001. The tower was one of three. It allowed various emergency response agencies to communicate and

Tony on Richmond Tower - photo by Vicky Kaseorg

coordinate their efforts. Prior to the Smart Zone system, the firemen, police, and medics all had separate systems with very little overlap in communication. The Smart Zone system is expensive to install, and not all cities can afford such an investment. However, it vastly improves the emergency response system of the city.

The project manager, Fred Hughes, was a kind man who had retired, but came out of retirement at times for special projects like the Smart Zone. He had a grandfatherly demeanor, and was soft spoken. He told me that prior to this project, he had known little about towers, but had learned a great deal when the Smart Zone system was installed. He spent quite a quite a while proudly telling me about the tower and the significance of the project.

"We can see one of the other towers that communicates with this one from the edge of the parking lot. Would you like to see?"

He walked me a hundred feet across the parking lot. Then he pointed at the distant skyline of Richmond, about three or four miles away. He identified some landmarks, and then City Hall.

"See the monopole on top of City Hall? That's the second tower. It has to have a straight line of sight to this one," he explained.

That day, the tower erectors would be installing braces around the portions of the legs that needed shoring up to withstand the stresses additional equipment would place on them. Fred was most concerned about the reinforcements that would be needed near the microwave dish. He explained that in order to strap the braces on, the attachment of the microwave dish would need to be loosened. The microwave was positioned in exactly the proper position such that it lined up perfectly with the microwave on the tower atop City Hall that I had just seen. If it shifted during the bracing operation, it could

Tony in gear - photo by Vicky Kaseorg

have devastating results. No one yet knew how much, if at all, it was likely to shift during the operation. Tony suited up in the tower climber's safety equipment to scale the tower and assess how to best protect the

Looking up center of Richmond Tower - Photo by Vicky Kaseorg

microwave and attach the braces.

The climber's safety equipment looked like it weighed more than Tony. Straps were attached all around his body, and there were two hooks on cables that he would use to attach himself to the tower. He looked like a Super Hero -- a super hero with a camera. At all times, one of those hooks should be attached to the tower. When changing position on the tower, one hook would be detached and placed in the new position, but the other hook would still be attached so that if the climber should stumble, he could not fall.

If the safety procedures were followed 100% of the time, there would be few mishaps on towers. The overwhelming reason for tower erecting having the dubious honor of being the "world's most dangerous occupation" is because the workers do not always follow those safety precautions. However, Tony followed the safety procedures which explained why he was still around to celebrate his 53rd birthday.

I arrived that morning when the crew hoped to begin their work. It was a perfect day for tower erecting, or really any kind of work outdoors. The sun was shining, and a cool breeze kept the seventy-degree day from being too hot. The sky was an uninterrupted blue, save for a hawk floating above the tower, and flocks of birds occasionally winging by. It would have been peaceful had it not been for the deafening roar of heavy equipment coming from the City Public Works operation complex just on the other side of the tower field. The crew had not yet begun work, so I was allowed to stand near the base of the 400-foot, self supporting tower.

Looking straight up from the center of the tower base, cross beams interlaced like geometric art. The sun glinted off the metal. The tower seemed to spin a little against the cerulean blue, but it may have been viewer vertigo.

The crew was gathered and ready but unfortunately, the large truck with the heavy steel reinforcement pieces was unable to drive into the narrow lot beside the tower. The crew had to scramble and solicit a nearby forklift to come over from the noisy plant next door.

The forklift made several trips, tediously carrying a few pieces at a time from the truck to the tower site.

Meanwhile, Hunter explained the crew's various roles. He himself would operate the "hoist." This was the machine that rolled out the cable that would be raised to the top of the tower. The workers would secure the cable, and through a pulley system, the load could then be raised or lowered as needed on the cable. Additionally, the hoist operator would be responsible for attaching and monitoring the "tag line."

The tag line pulled the cable away from all the obstructions it would encounter on its ascent up the tower. The tower is covered with lights, ladders, microwave dishes, and other equipment. If the cable and its load were to catch and snag along the way, not

Tony showing how tag line works - photo by Vicky Kaseorg

only could it ruin the sensitive equipment, but could potentially bring down the tower. The hoist operator

170

had a crucial role in protecting the safety of the crew, the equipment, and the tower.

Hunter's wife, Kelly, had begun as a secretary in the tower business. She had advanced to understanding all aspects of the process and would spend part of the day operating the hoist. She told me that the most important thing was to "pay attention," the same mantra I heard continually from Tony.

It was not difficult to operate the hoist, though of course required training, but she said she could never lose sight of the fact that people's lives were in her hands. Depending on what task they were busy accomplishing, they were continually alerting Kelly to lower the cable, or raise it. Since equipment was attached to the cable, any miscalculation could certainly result in damage if not to the tower, then to the tower workers. There was frequent chatter back and forth over the headsets. Once the cable was hoisted, and the riggers were on the tower, Kelly never took her eyes off them. I am not sure she even blinked. She most certainly was "paying attention."

Before the cable was hoisted, a crew member buckled on the labyrinth of straps and carabineers required to safely crawl up the tower. He began to ascend, using pegs sticking out from each leg of the tower – the climber's ladder. He moved slowly up the tower, pausing only for brief periods, growing smaller and smaller against the vast blue backdrop of the perfect sky.

Tony explained the process. First, the climber went up to "rig the tower." That meant he laboriously climbed step by step to the top of the tower with a rope trailing behind him. The rope would be used to pull the cable up later with the hoist. The cable itself was far too heavy for a worker to haul up, though sometimes if there was a large enough crew, that could be done. Sometimes, workers avoid subsequent tedious climbs by "riding the line." This means they are hoisted up the tower by the cable. They can also come down by this method, slowly lowered while attached to the cable.

I settled myself on a nearby hillside to watch the rigging. A black cat wandered in the tall grass beneath the tower. While the cat prowled after whatever little creatures lurked beneath the massive tower, the tower erector kept climbing. A flock of birds startled from their tower perch 200 feet in the air, and with a flurry of wings, abandoned their posts. The man kept climbing while the birds fluttered beneath him. From where I sat on the hillock, he looked as small as a bird himself. As he continued upward, a hawk circled on the thermals just above him.

"He hates those," Kelly told me. Other crew members told me that the hawks sometimes dive bombed if they had a nest nearby. The birds also were messy, a fact any parakeet owner could corroborate. It was difficult at times for the climber to find untainted handholds.

Finally, the climber ascended almost to the top where he attached the rope and pulley. My neck ached, craning to watch him so far up in the air. While the crew below barked directions into the walkie-talkies they used to communicate, the climber lowered one end of the rope. It often got hung up on crossbars and equipment on the way down, but from his vantage point at the top, he couldn't see that. The people below instructed him to jiggle the rope, raise it, lower it quickly, pull it back up, and swing it. There was a lot of shouting and gesticulating from below, until finally, it safely made it to the ground.

The cable now needed to be hoisted. The end of the rope was attached to the cable and Hunter settled in place on the hoist seat. While he watched as carefully as the hawk that was circling the tower, he turned on the noisy engine and began letting out the cable. A crew member at the base of the tower helped guide the cable slowly up. Once the cable was in place, the forklift had not yet delivered all the braces. The climber still waited, 400 feet in the air.

"What's he doing up there? Just hanging out? Talking on a cell phone?" I asked.

"Probably having a cigarette," said Kelly, "We discourage cell phones. For one thing, they are a distraction, and for another, you can drop them."

This day was a clear sunny day, not a cloud in the sky. However, tower workers do not always work in such ideal conditions.

"What happens if lightning strikes the tower while the workers are on it?" I asked Kelly.

She grimaced, and answered, "We try very hard to be sure they are not up there if a storm is rolling in."

"Would they be electrocuted?"

"No, but they would get a good shock. We don't stick around to find out. We monitor the weather ourselves, and watch the radar."

"And," added Tony, "you can see a storm coming in from miles away when you are up that high. You can actually see the bank of clouds where the front is, and the rain. When it starts to get close, you get off the tower."

"But you have to assess whether you can secure the equipment and just bring down the workers," said Kelly, "or does everything have to come down? It is a very time consuming task to get all that equipment up and then all of it back down. So you have to decide how much risk there is. And you hope you make the right call."

The taller the tower, the more tedious and time devouring the whole raising and lowering procedure becomes. Kelly said there were times they made the decision to batten the hatches and stay on the tower, and it was pretty dicey. She scowled and furrowed her forehead explaining the gut wrenching decisions they sometimes had to make.

While we waited for the equipment to be delivered, Kelly and Hunter both sang Tony's praises.

"Most engineers never come to the field, and they certainly never climb the tower," she told me, "Tony is always here, always making suggestions, and helping."

Later, with typical modesty and respect, Tony told me that he never tried to second guess the tower erectors. They were the experts and he trusted they knew what they were doing. However, he would watch and listen carefully, and try to find ways that he could help make their job easier through his engineering.

"For example?" I asked, "Can you be specific?"

"Well," said Tony instantly, kicking at one of the steel supports at our feet, "this hole here in the support allows them to hoist the steel with a hook, instead of just strapping it. That is easier, and safer."

Prior to that single hole being drilled into the support beam, it was hauled up the tower by carefully wrapping it with the straps, and then hooking the cable to the straps. The workers had to be very careful to be sure the straps were tight enough that the beam would not work loose. The hole Tony suggested be drilled in the brace beam eliminated a step in the tedious process, and added a degree of safety.

Such a simple, common sense solution to something they may never have even noticed was a problem! And if Tony did not take the time and effort to be at the work site, the simple solution might never have occurred to him. Remarkably, when asked for a specific example, he didn't need to look further than a few feet away to produce an immediate response. That would suggest there were many examples of time saving, safety enhancing modifications that this conscientious engineer on site had been able to implement.

Finally, the last load of structural supports was delivered by the forklift, which only took out two or three branches of a nearby tree as it tried to maneuver into the tight spot. The erector who had been waiting with his cigarette atop the tower had finally bored of the rarified air and come down. But now it was time to head back up the tower and get to work. I was told to put on my hard hat as now things could fall on me.

Both climbers ascended to the spot where the first brace would be installed. Step one involved cutting off the pegs that stuck out for the climbers to step on. The braces could not be strapped on till the pegs were removed. Sparks flew off of the pegs and each time one would finally shear away from the tower, they would call out, "Headache!"

"Know why they are yelling that?" asked Tony.

I smiled, nodding while the oversized hard hat he had loaned me clanged about on my head. I imagine those sheared pegs falling a few hundred feet would give a pretty nasty concussion, let alone a headache.

I was sitting on the tail gate of a pick-up truck with Tony and Fred, all three of us swinging our legs and chatting while watching the tower riggers. Fred stood, and peered a little worriedly at the base of the tower.

Tony understood immediately what concerned Fred. "It's ok, I heard it fall," he said, "and I've been watching. I don't think it is dry enough to worry."

The pegs would get quite hot, as the metal was burned away. Had the conditions been dryer, the hot metal could have started a fire in the tall brush beneath the tower. I hoped the cat had left the premises.

"I thought I saw it land on a cross bar, but I didn't see it come down," Fred said.

"I heard it land," said Tony, "But I will go check that." He went right over and prowled around till he found the peg. He returned and assured Fred all was well.

The rest of the afternoon was spent watching the workers shear off the pegs. Kelly now spelled Hunter at the hoist seat, and she never took her eyes off the erectors. They would squawk through the walkie-talkie when they needed the cable to be raised or lowered and she never let her attention waiver.

By 5:00, quitting time, they had not proceeded as far as they had hoped due to the delays of the truck delivery. I never did get to see the structural braces set in place, strapped securely on, and the final careful adjustment of any equipment that had to be displaced. I was sorry to have to leave without seeing the finished job. The climbers made their way back to earth.

One of the climbers had been erecting towers for fifteen years, the other only for two.

"Are you ever scared?" I asked.

"Yes," said the young man of two-years' experience, "But it's good to be scared. You *should* be scared."

The veteran climber just shook his head.

"But is it fun?" I asked.

The young man smiled at me, "It's a *blast!*"

The older rigger averted his eyes, not seeming anxious to share his story. I wondered if some of his stories were not glorious.

CHAPTER SIXTEEN
A Towering Coincidence

If only the WBT-AM beacon could talk, tell me its story. It may have been an airmail beacon, but the proof of that was not conclusive. It was clearly a WWII-era beacon, and most of the folklore regarding its function assumed a role in the war. What might that role have been? The chief engineer of WBT-AM was not very interested in speculating. He said that anyone that could answer my questions first hand was gone, as in *dead*. Understanding his reticence in speculating, I asked if he would be willing to confirm factual information, such as the size of the beacon, its make and model, and whether it flashed only red?

He offered that the next time he was on the transmitter building roof, he would measure the beacon. He did not intimate this was a regular occurrence. I think he considered me a pest.

A discussion group at the 'Pilots of America' website yielded interesting ideas. One discussion thread was titled, "How did WWII pilots do it?" This group was comprised of pilots, and many of them who answered the query were WWII aviators. Some suggested that the success of WWII pilots was partially due to luck. Many perished in training, and many died or were lost and missing during the war. Navigation instruments by today's standards were like lighting a fire with flint and a stick. They relied heavily on a compass, land clues, and when possible, *radio signals*!

My new friend, the online beacon expert John Eney, explained how radio signals might be used if a pilot was very far away from the transmitter. When an airplane is very high, the curvature of the earth doesn't hide distant waves -- both light and sound. Therefore, a radio signal could be detected from great distances. It was quite likely that pilots over the Atlantic, lost and fumbling for direction cues, *could hear distant radio signals.*

During the war years, the WBT-AM beacon and towers were in empty farmland. There were few lights in the unpopulated pastureland southeast of Charlotte. The setting appeared to be ideal for the tower signals to transmit huge distances, and for the beacon to be visible as well.

John Eney also mentioned that airway beacons had specially coded flashes, in accordance with Morse code. Along the air routes, the codes spelled phrases that pilots would remember and thus helped them follow the beacon path in proper order.

This was interesting but posed another conundrum. Rotating beacons were not the ones that flashed a course code. There were smaller "directional" or course beacons that fulfilled that role. Yet as far as I knew, WBT-AM only had the one rotating beacon on the roof.

Another post in the 'Pilots of America' website observed that many planes were lost during WWII due to the still archaic navigation aids available at the time. Many of the pilots described the almost desperate reliance on *distant radio signals* to guide them. It may not have been ideal, but over water or in unfamiliar territory, or at night, those distant radio signals might have been their only hope. Or they may have been the Germans sending up signals to confound them.

*****

The WBT-AM historian agreed that in the days of unrestricted clear channel broadcast, before the 1970s, troops in Europe and all over the country could hear WBT-AM. Several internet blurbs mentioned wartime Navy sailors thrilled to hear the voice of Grady Cole on WBT-AM from Charlotte. If they could *hear* WBT-AM, then the signal could be available to pilots to navigate upon as well.

"Anything in the archives about a lost WWII pilot finding his way home on a WBT-AM beam?" I asked the WBT-AM historian, sending up a brief prayer.

He could not recall any.

I felt that the growing evidence of the towers' potential role in aiding wartime navigation had to produce clues as to the function of the beacon.

James Peters suggested I contact another war pilot he knew. James thought perhaps that pilot would know something about flying on commercial radio beams and said he had a story of getting lost over the ocean. He didn't have a phone number for the pilot, Jules Horowitz, but did have an email address.

I wrote to Jules, "When you got lost over the ocean...you didn't happen to find your way home on a WBT-AM Charlotte radio beam, did you?"

*****

WBT-AM may or may not have been useful in wartime navigation, but radio beams certainly played pivotal roles in the war. One of the most diabolical uses of radio in the war became known as "The Battle of the Beams." The Germans quickly discovered that flying bombers during daylight hours allowed the enemy ample opportunities to shoot them down. They decided to put their energy into innovative new radio flying techniques that would allow them to navigate at night and zero in on blacked out targets with astonishing precision. Essentially, radio transmitters were set up at two points in Germany and each directed their radio beam to the target. Where the beams intersected was the point where the bombers were to drop their payload. They followed the first radio beam while listening for the sounds of the second radio. As the second became stronger, they tried to balance between the two sounds, and where they converged, the sound made a steady hum which was the cue for the bombardiers to let loose.

The British figured out what the Germans were doing, and used a code name for the beam system -- "headache." Struggling to counteract the Germans, they finally devised a simple, elegant solution, code-named "aspirin." The British simply sent up counter beams that confused the pilots so they would think the beams crossed somewhere else. The confuzzled German pilots would drop their bombs wherever the British radio engineers wanted them to. Some German pilots then landed at British Air-Force bases, thinking they were following the beam safely back to Germany.

More complicated and elaborate beam navigation ensued, but in the end, the British so confounded the

Germans, that they lost all faith in radio navigation, and aborted their efforts at night bombing. This was poetic justice, given what the Germans were doing with false radio beams, luring Allied pilots to their grave.

Happily, radio waves could and were used for life-saving, constructive purposes as well. Even nowadays, pilots' instruments can malfunction, and if visibility and weather conditions are abominable, the result can often be loss of level flight, disorientation, and finding oneself in too intimate contact with a mountainside. In an article by Thomas G. Lusch, a private pilot, the Benefits of ADF (Automatic Direction Finder) were extolled should one find oneself lost and struggling in inclement weather with defunct equipment.

In fact, The Space Shuttle pilots insisted that NASA install ADF instruments in the shuttle Columbia. With all the astonishing navigation tools on those shuttles, the pilots wanted WWII technology, ADF, in case of emergencies. NASA complied.

The Radio navigation using ADF is inexact and not as good as modern instruments, but when the instruments fail, homing in on a *commercial radio beam* can be good enough to keep the wings level and find one's way.

There are airway beams specifically designed to aid pilots called Navigation Directing Beacons (NDB), but they are weaker than powerful commercial AM stations and therefore, at times, insufficient to aid the hapless pilot. Furthermore, the best AM stations to use for this sort of navigation in emergencies are *distant* stations with highly powerful ranges. If the pilot is too close to the station, it is not able to guide him in keeping level.

Lusch said the best stations are those that operate at 50,000 watts twenty four hours a day. In 1990, when the article was published, there were 140 stations in the USA and Canada that fit the bill. While not necessarily a perfect solution, the author said, "If one receives a reasonably strong signal that produces a steady ADF needle, it has the potential of being a beacon of hope for the unlucky pilot." (Lusch, ADF)

Then the author listed those 140 stations that operated at 50,000 watts 24 hours a day. WBT-AM Charlotte was one of the stations lauded as a beacon of hope for the desperate pilot, lost and seeking a beam to guide him on level wings to safety.

On August 12th, 1932, WBT-AM officially switched on their new 50,000-watt transmitter. August 12th was declared WBT-AM-Charlotte day in 1932, with gala events surrounding WBT-AM's launch as an elite member of one of the nation's few super power radio stations. As of August 12, 1932, that 50,000-watt station clearly met all the necessary parameters of an AM station that the luckless pilot *could* use to guide him when all other navigational aids failed.

*****

Jules Horowitz the Pilot wrote back while I was busily concocting my wild scenarios, that seemed less wild by the moment.

"I was lost while training as a cadet. That is a good story in itself. But I didn't fly back on radio beams."

In fact, he never flew on radio beams in Europe. They were rarely available, and when they were, they were unreliable. He did learn to navigate using radio direction while training in the United States. He had no idea why the beacon might have been at WBT-AM though he recalled using beacons to mark flight position in the United States.

*****

Surprisingly, the Smithsonian not only wrote back, but one of their aviation experts exchanged emails with me. He speculated that the WBT-AM towers may have helped a WWII pilot navigate, but it would be impossible to find or corroborate. It would be like finding a needle in a haystack. He felt that if such an incident had occurred, it might be reported back to a superior officer but not likely to be entered as an official document that would be archived in the Smithsonian. Should they become lost, he reminded me, WWII pilots had other sources of navigation. They would have used celestial navigation, dead reckoning, and airborne radio direction finders.

*****

Undeterred, I sent a picture of the WBT-AM beacon to the *Friends of the Beacon Field Airport* in Maryland.

"Is this an airmail beacon?" I asked.

"No," they wrote back, "Too small and too low."

They insisted that if the beacon were mounted on a low building, planes would fly too low and crash into the building. While the official airmail beacons were mounted on tall towers, beacons had been placed every ten miles for airmail navigation. "Were they *all* mounted on towers?" I asked the *Friends of Beacon Field Airport*, "Might they be placed on buildings along the route similar to the WBT-AM transmitter building?"

No. They guessed that the beacon was a promotional searchlight, of the sort radio stations were wont to use in the mid 1900s.

The beacon that I had spent countless hours researching was like the colored flags lining used car lots, drawing in potential customers? (*Just stab a dull knife in my heart. Poke my eyes out with a feather duster. Remove my brain with an icepick up my nose.*)

After recovering from my collapse over the exchange with the *Friends of Beacon Airport*, I discovered a fascinating web page by Steven Wolff filled with information on the old airmail system. Steven Wolff is a retired airline pilot who has a wealth of information on many historic aviation sites. He offered to research his data base for the specific airmail beacon positions. However, he insisted that the beacons used in the airmail system had been largely dismantled, and found it highly doubtful that the WBT-AM beacon was involved in any kind of federal airway.

Alternatively, he felt it was possible beacons had been installed for private aircraft, not part of the federal airway system. My beacon may still have been used to guide airplanes, but he thought it could also be a spotlight. He did not believe it was a navigational beacon.

He agreed it was possible it might have been used to point the way to an airport. Was there an arrow on the roof? I had considered the very same thing. I had written to the WBT-AM chief engineer (again), but he didn't know if there had been an arrow at one time, and didn't wish to speculate (again). The roof had been painted many times over the years, and if an arrow had been there once, it would be impossible to know for sure. I uncovered old aerial photos of the area, but they were too grainy and indistinct to discern if an arrow was on the roof. I did detect a possible goat in the field.

Steven promised to look again at the CAM beacon maps. However, when I badgered him about the possibility of the towers' roles in guiding WWII pilots, he told me politely that I was barking up the wrong transmitter. He said AM stations would only be used in "homing" in on a curve. Besides, they would be as useful to the enemy as to the good guys, so he felt sure Allied pilots would not have used the radio beams to find their way home.

Contrary to what Steven was telling me, I had found evidence that commercial radio beams could and were used in emergencies. It may not have been the first choice but surely a desperate pilot running out of gas over the ocean would search for something to direct him to shore.

In fact, Wikipedia noted that radio direction flying, which was in use right before and during WWII, was a critical component of navigation. It specifically stated that commercial AM radio stations were required to broadcast their station identifier in part to aid both boat and plane navigation (ADF, Wikipedia)

Steven did some more digging and found just what John Eney had told me. An Air Commerce flight map showed a beacon at WBT-AM in 1937. Steven promised to find who installed it and when. If it was a federal airways beacon, it would have been licensed and the records should be available about this star of wonder, star of might, star of ancient beauty bright…

CHAPTER SEVENTEEN

A Towering Devotion

Tony's daughter, Starr was the only thing he spoke of with more delight than of tower building. Starr is well named. She grew into a glowing, beautiful young woman, with wavy dark hair, and sultry, smoky, dark eyes. Her smile is as guileless, open, and engaging as her father's. Starr, a junior in 2012 when I first met her, attended the College of Charleston. She wasn't yet sure what she wanted to do with her life upon graduating with her Spanish Major and International Studies Minor.

"Why those majors?" I asked, "What do you hope to do?"

"Honestly," she said, "I hope to go to Spain and find a husband so I can stay in Spain."

That is one way to interpret International Studies!

Starr was forthright, honest, and sincere, just like her father. She didn't try to impress me, therefore I was completely impressed. She was a lovely young lady with no airs or affectations, who loved her father unabashedly

"Did you ever consider engineering yourself?" I asked.

"Oh no!" she laughed, "I am horrible at math! That is one way that I am not like my father at all! I majored in Spanish because it was easy for me."

Starr, like Tony, was fluent in Spanish. After the divorce, with their yearly trips to Spain, Starr fell in love with the people and the culture.

"I think they have the right perspective," she told me, "They take siestas every day, and they make time for family. They always come home for dinner together. They seem to have a better understanding of what really matters."

I asked Starr what we should know about her father. She told me he was extremely hard working and dedicated. She returned to the theme of his dedication to work several times during our discussion.

"Sometimes I worry about him," she admitted, "I know he loves what he does, but I worry that he never really relaxes. I mean he does so little for himself. He will do anything for anybody, very caring and such a good friend. And he made time for me, even more so after the divorce. We travelled every summer. But he works so many hours. I just worry that he doesn't do enough for himself."

In Starr's view, the work ethic was a double-edged sword. She grew up knowing that her father travelled constantly, that he would not be around much. When he was around, he was a loving and gentle father, fun and always full of surprises. Even through the marriage collapse, she remembers him as unfailingly kind to her.

But Starr told me that when the marriage ended, there was a slow change in her relationship with her father. She remembered the relationship as always being a good one. She did not allude to a period when she was distancing herself from him. Whatever confusion she had felt as a young teen enduring the breakup, she seemed to have now resolved. But after the divorce, she felt her relationship with her father became even closer.

Now single, Tony became increasingly attentive, always made time for her, and always made sure that their days together were joyous. Starr was eager to point out that he had always been a good father, and had been available for her when he was home, even before the divorce. But he was rarely home.

The breakup of the marriage, the dissolution of Kline, and the period of overwhelming loss did not keep Tony down. As surely as he had rebuilt the WBT-AM towers after the hurricane, he now began to rebuild the life he wanted with his daughter. After leaving Kline, enduring the three acquisitions, then working at yet another engineering firm in remote contract work, and finally becoming a partner at Turris Engineering Inc, he steadily built upon the strong foundation he'd spent a lifetime cementing, for himself and his daughter to reconnect.

"I loved my family in Spain," Tony told me, "One of the problems in the marriage was my former wife didn't like my family. It was something that was so important to me, and so that was a difficult strain. I am so glad that Starr has connected so strongly with her heritage. I worried that she might not have."

"Every vacation or holiday time we would travel, after the divorce," she told me, "He had so many frequent flyer miles that we would go all over the place.

And nearly every summer we would go see my family in Spain. Since the divorce, I have become even closer to him. Now I talk with him almost every day."

Tony was a father who led not only with his words but by example. Whenever they would pass a homeless person, or someone selling goods for a living on the streets, Tony never failed to buy their product or offer them money.

"And he has millions of quotes he is always saying!" laughed Starr, "Like he used to tell me, 'Give a man a fish, and he eats for a day. Teach a man to fish and he eats for a lifetime.' He used to recite the Serenity Prayer, but he would say it in Spanish. You know, the one that goes: God grant me the serenity to accept the things I cannot change. The courage to change the things I can, and the wisdom to know the difference.

"And he would say, 'If you don't ask, you will never know,' or another one of his sayings was, 'There is no short-cut without a lot of work.' He is really fun. He is all about surprises. He is always trying to surprise someone; there is always something up his sleeve. Like once he made us think we were going somewhere else in Spain, and we ended up on a plane to Paris!"

"Did you ever climb a tower?" I asked.

"Well once he took me to a tall tower, high above the city. It was on top of a tall building. We stood up there, way above the city, and he knew where everything was. He pointed to all the parts of the city. I am not usually afraid of heights, but that time I was a little nervous. It was very high, on top of that tall building."

"Did it ever worry you, the danger of your father's work?"

"Not when I was little. I didn't really understand. But when he took me to the top of that building, to see that tall tower, for the first time, I really had a sense of what he does every day, and how dangerous it is. Now it *does* worry me. I know he is careful and he has done this his whole life, so I have to just trust that he will be ok, but yes, it worries me."

I asked her if during the very hard and trying times of the divorce he ever lost patience, ever expressed his frustration, or ever raised his voice.

"I can count on one hand the number of times he ever raised his voice. He is very emotional, I mean, he will cry at a movie, but he never got mad. He never raised his voice to me. He was always even-keeled and patient. I wish I were more like him in that way. I am more impatient.

"He didn't scream, but he would motivate me....I don't want to say with 'bribes', but more like rewards for doing the right thing or doing well in school. Like I would tell him things I wanted to do, and he would say that we could do that on certain conditions, like that I would get good grades. But he would never tell me anything that he didn't tell himself. When I would tell him I wanted to do something, but it was hard, he would tell me stories about things that he did that were hard but how he would work through it. I think he told you he is a runner, and he would tell me things like, 'I wanted to decrease my time and so on that last mile, I made myself run a minute faster...' Things like that. He led me by example, not just talk. Oh, and he used to say, 'Don't play catch up, play keep up!' He said stuff like that all the time.

"He was always an encourager, always compassionate, and selfless and giving. He does almost nothing for himself. The only thing is his triathlons. He is really good at that. He usually places first or second or third in his age group. And if he doesn't, he is really disappointed in himself."

"Do you like to run too?" I asked.

"No," she said emphatically, "That is one way we are not alike at all! I hate exercise!"

Did this paragon of fatherhood have any weaknesses? Much as I admired Tony, I was beginning to hate him.

"Yes," said Starr, "Neither he nor I easily brush off hurt feelings. I guess we are over sensitive. And I think he overworks. That is both a good and bad thing. I also worry that he is too stressed, but he doesn't show it."

Starr felt that Tony, like so many of us, struggled to maintain a healthy work and family time balance. He had dated sporadically over the years, but never found anyone so special that he would want to settle into marriage again. He worked too much, Starr thought, with little down time. She noted that he had improved over the years, but contrary to Tony's opinion on the matter, she felt it contributed to the breakup of the marriage.

Despite the dire statistics regarding children of divorce, Starr seemed to be remarkably intact. She had a great love and respect for both her parents, maturity and understanding beyond her years, respect, kindness, and a sense of fun, delight, and wonder at all the possibilities of life. She felt the ideal job would be in fashion and travel, and then echoed her father, "I know I don't want to sit in an office every day."

"I owe everything to my dad," she told me, "It's his fault! He showed me so much of the world, and now, I just want to see more! I want to see what else is out there! How can I just stay here in South Carolina? He gave me this lust to travel, to see new things. I pretend I am a spoiled brat, and ask him why he gets to travel first class but not me? But really, I am just kidding. He has given me everything. I appreciate so much what I have. And I owe it all to him."

He had not rebuilt the marriage. But the engineer *had* rebuilt his life and carried his daughter in his capable arms aloft with him to look out over the horizon and thirst for distant lands. They had scanned the horizon together, and hand in hand, sought it. It was perplexing to me that such an accomplished, loving, and attractive man had never remarried. All his hopes for an eternal union seemed to have been sublimated to the strong relationship with his daughter. Still, I wondered if he ever ached with the absence of 'the one.'

*****

Tony and Starr paused in a small store from their wanderings through the streets of the family hometown in Spain. It was a little gift shop, and Starr and her friends delightedly fingered the Spanish shawls, and beautiful jewelry. They watched as Tony examined a bracelet and then brought it to the counter to pay for it.

"Who's that for?" asked Starr.

"Someone special that I will meet someday," said Tony, his perennial optimism bubbling again to the surface.

CHAPTER EIGHTEEN
A Towering Proof

My optimism was bubbling to the surface as well. True to his word, Steven sent me scans from the U.S. Dept of Commerce that showed exactly what I had hoped and speculated about so many months now. In 1931, Charlotte was not directly on the CAM 19 route, but was a spur, labeled C1 on the Federal Airways Map. A beacon was at a site called the Charlotte airport, but there was nothing yet at the WBT-AM site. The first tower had not yet been built, though the transmitter building was there by 1931. The second scan Steven sent me showed that in 1937, WBT-AM was listed as part of the airway system with a red rotating beacon, and two coded beacons as well. Coded beacons! That was just what John Eney had indicated were used in the airmail system to point pilots on the correct path with Morse code flashes. What happened to those two coded beacons?

According to the 1937 information, the WBT-AM station had a 24 inch rotating red beacon, with the two coded beacons as well, likely pointing the way to the landing field at the Charlotte Airport. Tower A was built by that time, but not the other two towers yet. Steven told me he felt the WBT-AM beacon was probably built by either Westinghouse or Sperry, and had to have been installed sometime after 1931, but before 1937. He affirmed that the code beacons were often used along airways with coded flashes to help the pilot determine his position. (Wolff, Federal Airway System)

Charlotte.—Charlotte Airport, commercial. Three and one-half miles NW. from center of city; reservoir one and one-half miles N. Lat. 35°14'; long. 80°54'. Alt. 750 feet. Irregular, 2,000 by 2,700 feet, clay, grass, and gravel, level, natural and artificial drainage; three runways, 2,500 by 300 feet NW./SE., 2,000 by 450 feet NE./SW., 2,300 by 300 feet N./S.; entire field available. Steel tower and high tension line 1½ miles S., trees to NW., SE., and W.; pole line 400 feet W.; 430-foot antenna tower 8 miles SSE. of field marked by 24-inch red rotating beacon and two code beacons, obstructions lighted; 94-foot antenna tower 3¾ miles SE., obstruction lighted, grand stand to NW., within boundary marker. CHARLOTTE AIRPORT on hangar with N. arrow. Beacon, boundary, approach, and landing area floodlights. Beacon, 24-inch rotating, clear. U. S. Weather Bureau maintains an office at the airport. Facilities for servicing aircraft, day and night. Teletypewriter. Radio marker beacon, call WWIS, identifying signal "H" (. . . .), operating frequency 248 and 365 kcs. Lights operated for scheduled landings and upon request only.

Descriptions of Airports and Landing Fields in the United States, US Dept of Commerce, Jan. 1, 1937. WBT-AM is the 430' antenna noted with rotating beacon and two coded beacons.

"You need to find a pilot who flew on WBT-AM beams," added Steven.

I laughed. He appeared to be completely on my side now. I wrote to the Air-force but they suggested I contact the Army. The media relations receptionist was very kind and helpful. She listened to my request and surprisingly didn't hang up on me. In fact, she gave me three different departments and names of sources she felt might be able to help me. She told me if they couldn't help me find my lost pilot, call her back and she would help me come up with another plan. I wrote to them all immediately. One wrote back and told me it was certainly possible to fly on AM radio beams, and he knew the Japanese and American forces had done so en route to Oahu. He also mentioned the fallibility of doing so, citing the *Lady Be Good* episode of the plane overshooting the station it had been homing on, and running out of gas far beyond the base. He had heard of no other stories, but assured me, that didn't mean they weren't out there.

Steven, hot on the trail now, called me with more perplexing information. He had perused ten years of Department of Commerce bulletins regarding beacon and airfields from 1929-40, and there was no mention of licensing the WBT-AM beacon. He concluded, they had not licensed it with the Federal system, nor as far as he could see, *any* commercial licensing agency. This was highly irregular.

He found that in 1933, there was a private commercial airway from Charlotte to Augusta, Ga., that passed right over the WBT-AM station. He surmised the beacon was installed by that airline. However the airline only lasted two years. Many small airlines would spring up during that time period and many would have only one or two planes. Then they would go bankrupt and quickly fold.

He told me the airline only lasted two years, but the Airways route, first CAM 19, and then later Red 7 Airways, would have continued for some time. Red 7 was one of several color-coded airway routes that sprung up in the late 1930s. The Red 7 route roughly followed the CAM 19 path. However, he felt if the beacon were part of any airways route, it would have been licensed. He wondered about the course lights mentioned in the 1937 blurb about the WBT-AM beacon. Course lights were used to direct pilots.

Since the beacon was still there, perhaps the course lights were as well. I had to get on that roof somehow.

*****

In an online interview with Preston Bassett of the Sperry Company, he reminisced about the critical role the beacons had played in aviation history. Bassett surmised that it was the beacons, and the ability of Americans to learn all weather/ night flying that led to early air skills that no other country had yet developed. Those skills would be critical in WWII. Sperry Company had been responsible for developing many of the aircraft beacons, but he said the technology, significant in and of itself, gave rise to other important advances. Bassett said their work with beams led them to develop antiaircraft beams, critical in the war effort. Bassett was asked if the army had spearheaded the beacon project. Bassett said that it was actually the U.S. Lighthouse Bureau that oversaw the beacons. He pointed out that the Lighthouse Bureau had been using the technology of beacons and light in navigation for eons. It made sense that they would take over the lighting of airways as well.

After reading that, I fired off an email to the Lighthouse Bureau archive department. Another trail to follow! I asked them who installed the beacon atop the WBT-AM transmitter building, and when, and why.

*****

I begged the chief engineer at WBT-AM (again) to let me on the roof, but he wrote back saying it was impossible for many reasons, but he would go up there for me at some point. The response from the Lighthouse Bureau was similarly disappointing. They could possibly discover who installed the beacon, but it could take months of research into their archives and the research would be $50 an hour. I crossed the Lighthouse Bureau off my Christmas list.

*****

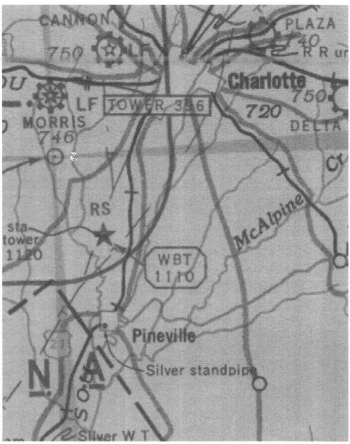

1939 Sectional showing red line denoting outer edge of Red 7 airways. Note WBT-AM marked by star showing beacon at site. Air Commerce Map

Then I received a disappointing email from Steven saying airway beacons are never red. They are always clear. The 1937 description of the WBT-AM Beacon as red ruled out any chance of it being an airways beacon. He felt certain it was a simple obstruction beacon.

This was contrary to what I found at an FAA site describing beacons. It clearly stated beacons could be red. I copied it and sent it to Stephen.

According to the FAA article, rotating airway beacons could be colored. Additionally, obstruction lights on towers were flashing white lights (like the Fresnel lens strobe I had seen in the transmitter building), and not rotating beacons. And finally, course lights were *only* installed for Federal Airways systems.

I sought clarification. Steven wrote back immediately, in a firm and convincing email. Basically, he told me I was wrong. Course lights could be colored, but never airway beacons. We exchanged several emails in battle over his contention that airways beacons are only clear, never red.

I prayed I was not annoying him to the breaking point with the dozens of emails fired back and forth. He seemed to have the patience of Job, and continued answering my questions. He felt the beacon marked the danger of the towers to airplanes, and the course lights probably marked the Red 7 airways which happened to turn north near the WBT-AM station. He sent a map of the Red 7 airways route. The outer edge of the airways turned northward right over WBT-AM. Coincidence?

Steven had noted that the 1937 document showed that both the beacon and the course lights were at WBT-AM, but in 1939, only the beacon was mentioned. Course lights, if present, would have been marked on the map. Where did they go? And why did they go there? The mystery was growing.

Steven seemed quite convinced that the rotating beacon was an obstruction light to warn pilots of the tower. He did not feel it was likely the Feds had installed it, though at this point, he was making no guesses about who *had* installed it. He insisted (again) airway beacons would be clear, not red.

I refused to give up. It is to Steven's credit that he did not block my emails or notify Homeland Security to put me on some watch list. The maps showed WBT-AM just inside the Red 7 airway, and it was right at the northward turn. It seemed reasonable to me that the beacon marked the turn. What added clout to this interpretation was that Red 7 was installed in 1937, the year the beacon was first mentioned, and thus likely the year it was installed. The aforementioned FAA publication had noted that course lights were used *ONLY* with rotating beacons of the Federal Airway system. It seemed incontrovertible to me that the beacon was indeed a navigational beacon of the Red 7 airway.

Steven reiterated the one problem with my theory -- the Federal Airway Beacons were clear. The WBT-AM Beacon was red. I asked him who besides the Feds would have installed course lights? He did give that question some thought. He still maintained the course lights were to warn of the towers, but was mulling over who but the Feds would have installed them. Not ready to abandon my theory yet, I asked him if it was just a coincidence that the Red 7 airway was installed the very same year the red beacon and the two course lights at WBT-AM appeared in official documents. He said we didn't really know if that was the first time they are mentioned, though I told him that John Eney had looked for any reference to them prior to 1937 and found none. Surprisingly, Steven didn't snap at my impertinence, but offered to explore the documents on his own.

Beacons and course lights were not cheap to build, install, or maintain. The most logical entity with money to pour into this elaborate system was the federal government. Could a red beacon be a signal for a turn? I knew at the least it was a signal that a landing field was not available at the site. Green denoted an acceptable landing field. Eastern Airlines flew right over Charlotte and may have had the money to install the beacon, but did private airlines install course lights? Not from what I had been able to discern from my research or from what Steven had told me.

I wondered if at some point, Steven would question why he was putting so much effort into such a seemingly inconsequential question. (Perhaps you are wondering that as well.) Having pursued the mystery this far, it was important to me to follow it through to the end. I hoped I didn't irritate Steven to the point that he took his data and slammed the door on me. My research would collapse without his input.

*****

Tony was ready to collapse, his life a never ending airplane trip to another job. He snatched the phone when it rang, and was happy to hear his sister's voice.

"Tony," said Sara, "There is someone I want you to meet. She is a fantastic person and single, not seeing anyone right now. I think you would really like her."

Tony, as always was racing from one job to another, with barely a moment in between to do the laundry and then dash off in a new direction.

"Tell me about her," he asked Sara, continuing in his packing for the trip out (again) the next morning.

So Sara told him about this woman, a dentist from Bosnia who had become one of Sara's close friends.

"Send me her picture," Tony said, the phone crunched against his ear as he zipped the suitcase he had just repacked.

"No," said Sara, "You need to meet her."

Tony paused, "Oh really? What are you hiding Sara?"

"Nothing," said Sara firmly, "She is gorgeous but that is not the point. I want you to see who she is inside, her character first. She is special, Tony. Really special."

"Sure Sara, I would love to meet this special woman!"

The dream that he had harbored of the perfect woman only came to him in the deep dark moments of the night when the tumult of life had stilled, and he would not remember the vision when he awoke. Not consciously. During wakeful hours, Tony knew only contentment, enthusiasm, reconciliation of his dreams with reality. Still, Sara's words stirred that quiet place inside that pictured a dark-haired beauty who could perhaps share his optimism and passion for life. Yes, he would like to meet this special woman.

But months went by without a break. Tony dashed from one job to the next, and yet another anniversary of the divorce and his years as a single man slipped by.

CHAPTER NINETEEN
A Towering Collapse

It was December 7, 1982, the 41st anniversary of the attack on Pearl Harbor. Another disaster would share that awful day, one that would also shower death from the sky. The TV/FM tower near Houston was almost 2,000 feet tall. It took months to build. As the workers gathered that morning, there was no premonition that a broken u-bolt would take it down, along with five workers, in 17 seconds. KTXH, a subsidiary of Fox, was a new station, only broadcasting for a year. The tower being constructed was nearing completion. The station was already operational using temporary antennas. They were eager to have the new tower completed.

It was a beautiful day, clear sky, perfect tower building weather. The already towering base, a uniform width tower, was secured by strong guy wires, and solidly in place beside the transmitter building. The huge flatbed truck arrived with the massive top mount panel antennas lashed atop the cargo bed. Workers excitedly swarmed over the truck bed, cutting away the lasts. Several microwave dishes were attached to the panel. The lifting lugs were configured such that the panel could be lifted horizontally from the truck bed.

However, to then turn the antenna vertically so it could be hoisted, the microwave dishes interfered with the action of the lugs. The construction company, Harris Construction, requested that the microwave dishes be removed, so they could safely lift the antenna panel. The design company, World Wide Towers, refused. Harris requested that World Wide design an extension arm that would allow the safe and necessary turn from horizontal to vertical. World Wide again refused. Therefore, Harris themselves designed an extension arm to lift the antenna that would not be impeded by the microwave dishes. They requested that World Wide Tower engineers look over and approve their design, but were refused again. World Wide Tower did not wish to accept the liability of work done by construction workers who were not professional engineers.

The lifting lug design was not adequate for the task required, yet the construction company was eager to move on with their job. Thus, the antenna was to be hoisted by an extension arm with u-bolts, never approved or designed by a professional engineer. The construction company used u-bolts and materials they had on site. Unfortunately, the u-bolts were designed to carry only about half the load weight of the antenna. Since it was all they had on site, it is what they used. It's likely a few fingers were crossed and prayers lifted as the antenna was hoisted.

Meanwhile, the riggers had scaled the base and carried the rigging line to the top where it was threaded over a pulley and lowered to the ground. The hoist cable was attached to the rope, raised, and secured.

Then the cable was lowered slowly and the attachment readied for the load it would haul to the top of the tower.

Several workers secured the u-bolts, and attached the tag lines. The top mount panel was to be raised in two sections. A station engineer was filming the exciting moment with a video camera. As the hoist line pulled the panel aloft, the camera captured its slow ascent.

The loud rumble of the hoist engine was difficult to talk over. The workers waiting on the tower wore headsets to communicate with the hoist operator. The camera scanned the distant hazy horizon. Downtown Houston could be seen several miles away, the tall buildings partially obscured in the haze. A few clouds wafted near the horizon, but the sky was otherwise empty and blue. Spirits were high. It was all going as planned, and was being captured on film. It was always a proud moment, the final stages of tower erecting. As the camera panned over the view, all looked peaceful, calm, and idyllic.

Next the camera settled on the group of tower riggers. They sat on the beams in a cluster. Some had no hard hats, perhaps having removed them as they rested to wait for the moment when they would be attaching the connection points. They smiled and waved, dangling their feet in the air, oblivious to the horrific fate that awaited them.

Below, the crew foreman sat at the hoist, watching carefully as the loud hum of the engine droned on. The cable was slowly let out; the tag line kept taut to keep the panel from striking the tower. Birds as always, flew near, occasionally pausing to rest on the new structure.

The workers, sitting on the beam laughed and chattered away, shading their eyes against the sun as they watched the panel slowly lifting upward. Everything was routine, done hundreds of times before. All was going well.

Though few people on earth could contemplate working so terrifyingly high above the earth and so fraught with danger, the tower workers were unconcerned. They were trained, and largely fearless. No one looking at the montage of their faces would suspect they were dangling some 800 feet in the air, sitting on a thin brace of metal. This was their work, and they loved it. The heights thrilled them. They knew they were brave, and were proud of their courage. The risks were always there, but they were strong, and young, and not worried. The danger was not worth dwelling on, and in fact, some felt cavalier about the risk, shedding the protective helmets and letting the breeze dance in their dark sweaty hair. They waved at the camera, jaunty machismo in their relaxed posture so frighteningly high above the ground.

The station was already operational, though the tower was incomplete. Two temporary antennas had been installed so that the station, KTXH could broadcast. As the new top antenna continued to inch its way up alongside the tower, the tag line was kept expertly taut. No jostling of the tower shaft or equipment could be allowed or it could take everything down.

The men on the ground watched carefully, doing their job exactly as specified. The panel only had perhaps a hundred feet to go when there was a sudden lurch. The camera operator yelled out, and the workers all froze. At first, none could believe what they were witnessing. They had done nothing wrong. All had been perfect. But now, with a terrifying shudder, the giant u-bolt snapped and the enormous top panel dropped like a spear flung by a giant. It smashed against the tower, throwing several of the workers through the air like missiles. On its disastrous plunge to earth, it smacked against a guy wire, severing it.

The camera man, running for his life as the tower came down, dropped the video camera. It landed on the ground in a puddle but continued recording. In the water's reflection, the snapping and collapse of the final guy wires was recorded, and then with an explosive shock, as the main tower came down, the camera was silenced.

When the main tower collapsed, the transmitter building was crushed. Wires, plaster, pieces of metal were strewn all across the field. Miraculously, the workers on the ground survived. Within minutes, rescue helicopters were roaring overhead. In the chaos, workers began ripping through the wreckage, hoping against hope that someone in that mess had survived.

Five workers were killed in the tower collapse. Three of the crew on the hoist and two on the tower died. All were under 26 years of age, some only 21-years old. Three others were injured from the collapse of the nearby building.

It was concluded that an extra "moment" (vibration) in the extension arm that it was not designed or able to compensate for, put too much stress on the inadequate u-bolt, and the u-bolt shattered. The bolt designer took full responsibility for the accident, having had previous issues with faulty bolts and not wanting their name to be sullied any longer than necessary. They settled quickly to avoid a drawn out inquiry. However, was the tower company faultless, with the inadequate lifting lug design? Should that have been their responsibility to alter? Was the construction company at fault for engineering an inadequate and poorly advised alternative with materials not meant to withstand the load?

The schedule and financial constraints of the construction business does not always put worker safety first. In the case of this tower collapse, there was more than enough blame to go around. Tony had graduated from The Citadel and been working on towers for about a year when the horrific accident occurred. No doubt, everyone in the tower construction world was impacted by the questionable ethics and incompetency that led to the deaths of so many young tower workers. Had just one person in any one of the major businesses connected with the construction of the tower stepped forward and challenged the series of events that led to such unfortunate decisions, those tower workers might still be alive.

Tony's father had always instilled in him respect for every worker that contributed to the whole. Tony had always valued every member of his team, from the chief engineer to the bolt maker. Everyone mattered to the success of the completed project, and the layers of trust were essential. He painfully found it true in marriage, as well as in his work. No foundation could be built on shifting sand, and as the Houston Tower proved, problems with a single bolt could collapse a tower.

*****

How did the aftermath of the tower collapse affect the way tower firms did business? Did OSHA change any rules as a result of the safety blunders along the way? Incredibly, the disaster in Houston occurred only 1 1/2 years after a very similar accident, where the same basic mistakes were made: Fast track design practices, divided responsibilities, and basic load calculation errors led to the collapse of the Hyatt Regency Skywalk in Kansas City, Missouri. That disaster was widely reported and scrutinized. Why were massive changes not made to prevent the same root causes from being responsible for yet another catastrophe? However, Tony told me we would need to discuss my questions in a few weeks. He was taking his daughter to Spain.

"Who would imagine my adult daughter would still want to travel with me?" he asked.

Earlier, when I had asked how he had built such a loving, trusting relationship with Starr, he sent me a poem. He said he first read it when Starr was still young, and had copied and framed it, and reread it often.

"It still brings tears to my eyes when I read it," he said, "She will not always be here, or want to come home. But I used to read that poem and remember how important it was to finger paint, not point fingers, affirm and not accuse...Especially as a single parent. It is easy to lose focus on what matters. You'll have to read it. I will send it to you."

The tower builder was not only good at raising *towers*. He knew that keeping trust was much easier than rebuilding it once it was shattered. Staying focused on what was important mattered in building towers and families. I wondered what those Houston tower workers would have done differently if they could do it all over again. But of course, they could not.

****

If I Had My Child to Raise Over Again
By Diane Boomans

If I had my child to raise over again,
I'd build self-esteem first, and the house later.
I'd finger paint more and point the finger less.
I would do less correcting and more connecting.
I'd take my eyes off my watch and watch with my eyes.
I would care to know less and know to care more.
I'd take more hike and fly more kites.
I'd stop playing serious and seriously play.
I would run through more fields and gaze at more stars.
I'd do more hugging and less tugging.
I'd see the oak tree in the acorn more often.
I'd be firm less often and affirm much more.
I'd model less about the love of power,
And more about the power of love.

*****

Tony drove contentedly home from the airport. It had been a grueling week, never a moment's rest. But characteristically, he was not complaining. He would never complain about being busy doing what he loved! He'd be traveling again in a day to his sister and Mom in New Jersey, combine it with a job in the City. But for now, he had a half day with no travel. He would grab the bike and do a much needed training ride. Maybe head along the lake...That would afford him time to think about what his sister Sara had said about this woman she wanted him to meet. Well, he'd met plenty of women. He could meet one more. He was past feeling disappointment.

His interest was piqued, however. The way Sara had described this friend, she really sounded too good to be true. He didn't want to get his hopes up. If she sounded too good to be true, she probably was. He had learned that the hard way. He would not enter the arena of relationships lightly ever again. He had trusted in love once, and it had led to years of heartache. Yes, he was stronger, but that kind of strengthening, he was happy to only endure once.

"I am content," he thought, "I need nothing more." The bracelet he had bought in Spain for a special someone sparkled in his dresser drawer.

He threw the suitcase on his bed. The tower gear duffle stayed in the car since he'd head back out in the morning.

"I'll unpack later," he said, "And then...repack."

Tony chuckled as he changed into his bike shorts and cleats. It was warm enough to just throw on a t-shirt. He headed to the basement where his beautiful bike leaned against the wall. His cleats clacked on the cement floor as he rolled the bike out the door. His phone rang. He grabbed it, saw it was a construction supervisor for the job he'd just left, and decided to let it go to voicemail. There were not many daylight hours left. As he pedaled through the quiet streets of his neighborhood, out to the main drag, he thought about what Sara had told him.

"This friend is great, Tony. I think you will really like her. I told her my brother was single and a great guy, and she is single and a great lady. No pressure. We'll just go to brunch and you can meet her."

She was a general and cosmetic dentist. Successful and smart. Sara had known her for years, first as a colleague, later as a dear friend. Their daughters roomed together in college. As it turned out, the two families lived just minutes from each other. They became very close friends, and shared their disappointments and heartbreaks in the midst of their successes and delights in life. Sara knew Tony had never found anyone he was willing to share his life with after the tremendous pain of the divorce and struggle with his former wife. He had been single for eight years now. Her friend Sanya had never met anyone she felt connected to at a deep enough level to ever consider marriage again after her own divorce.

"You just never know," Sara had told Tony, "You might hit it off."

As Tony pushed himself faster and faster on the bicycle, his breathing rhythmical but rapid, he thought about how blessed he was. He wanted for nothing. He had a great job, a great daughter, a beautiful home, engaging activities, and was the picture of health. He had long ago resolved himself to the fact that he was single, and likely to remain single. He could still picture his vision of the perfect woman, but he knew she existed only in his mind. European, dark-haired, similar to his own heritage. Smart, hard-working, accomplished, successful, beautiful, confident, sexy, healthy, and fit.

"Dream on!" he laughed. It was fine. Really it was. His life was perfect, and he would not complain. He pedaled till he felt his lungs would burst, exulting in stretching to the edge of endurance, and wondered about the lovely dentist.

*****

It had been in their thoughts for months, but now finally, it was set. Tony would be working in New York Friday night till the wee hours of Saturday morning. He would take the train to Sara's house in New Jersey and arrive Saturday, in time to meet the dentist, Sanya. He didn't know what Sara had planned, but she never did anything halfway. The drive for excellence ran deeply through the entire Fonseca brood.

After she told Tony the 'special' woman's name, he found her picture on her website. He sat down and peered at the head shot of the dark-haired beauty. Her eyes radiated kindness, and the pose was one of quiet confidence. Tony was hardly a shallow man, but the beautiful woman looked so familiar he could not rip his eyes away. He thought perhaps he knew her. But they had never met. He didn't realize that eerie sense of familiarity was his dream colliding with reality. That evening as he climbed the tower suspended so high above the earth, his thoughts were uncharacteristically *not* solely on the tower.

*****

The 'special' woman reread the email from Sara. Saturday morning! She was to meet the dashing engineer Saturday morning. She groaned as she looked at her flight itinerary. She would be flying back home during the wee hours of the night. How could she meet this special man Sara raved about with dark circles under her eyes and bleary half wakefulness after a night on the plane? Reaching for her phone, Sanya dialed the airline, and rebooked an afternoon flight. Yes, it was a pricey decision, but her thoughts were not on the money.

CHAPTER TWENTY
A Towering Pest

Follow the money. Maybe that was the way to solve the mystery. Eastern Airlines took over Pitcairn's airline and continued to deliver airmail along the CAM 19 route. Did they install beacons? While I did not find that information specifically, I did discover that all private airlines at the time were federally subsidized. None of them were able to remain financially sound until after WWII. Eastern Airlines was one of the more profitable and did manage to wean itself off government subsidy after the Second World War, but prior to that time, it accepted government help, specifically in running the airmail route. It seemed unlikely then that the airline installed the beacon, which I knew had been installed before Eastern was financially independent of government money.

Steven reread the 1937 document and realized it said code beacon, not course lights. I had known that, but assumed they were the same thing. They are not. "Now what did those code beacons flash?" asked Steven. He could not imagine why they were there. I knew the airmail system used code beacons but I went to the internet and found a company that sold code beacons. And I discovered a key fact, from the 1934

Communications Act, mentioned at that site. The Act required towers to have two code beacons.

The document described varying heights at which code beacons were required, but the code beacons could well be there to mark the tower. And two were required. The code beacons were on the tower, not the transmitter building. Thus, we were back to square one wondering about the reason for the rotating beacon. In all likelihood, the code beacons were there to mark the towers per the 1934 Communications Act. What did not make sense is why the code beacons were not mentioned as present after 1939. Why not? Another intriguing thought: If the code beacons were indeed present on the tower, as well as the top obstruction light, the rotating beacon was not likely yet *another* obstruction light, was it?

Again, Steven disagreed. He was adamant that airway beacons were clear only, never red. To tell you the truth, I was getting a little sick of this refrain. He did not believe the WBT-AM light was a navigational beacon. He said many private businesses and buildings had rotating beacons -- in fact, it became a source of contention for pilots as it was hard to discern the proper airway beacons when so many private beacons were flashing like lighted Christmas trees along their route.

What made no sense was that other towers were mentioned in the sectionals Steven had sent, but no others in the immediate area had either code beacons or rotating red beacons. If by 1934 all towers were required to have code beacons, why was the 94-foot tower right near the WBT-AM tower described as having obstruction lights, but no code beacons (or rotating beacon!)? And if it was a requirement of all towers, why mention it at all? It would be a given. Only the airport, other than WBT-AM, was described as having code beacons in the Charlotte area. I could not shake the feeling that the WBT-AM beacon was there for a purpose more critical than lighting the towers.

Red 7 pilots would fly right over WBT-AM, and the outer boundary of the jog from east-west to north occurred right over WBT-AM. Steven told me that pilots would fly on the outer edges of the airways rather than the middle to avoid head-on collisions. Was the beacon the last warning that pilots must turn now or lose the Red 7 path? And did the code beacons designate the turn direction?

Meanwhile, the general manager at WBT-AM was checking with his legal department to see if I could be allowed on the roof of the transmitter building. Steven told me to check the base of the beacon for numbers that would tell me the flash rotation rate. That would be very useful in determining why the beacon was there. I knew the airmail beacons had a standardized rotation rate, and I believe the Federal Airways beacons did as well. Nonetheless, Steven didn't buy my theory. He wrote his synopsis of the role of the beacon. It wasn't glorious, but I had to admit, it made sense. His summary: airways beacons are clear not red, would never be on a low building, and so the WBT-AM beacon was an obstruction beacon.

I wrote back, raising the white flag. Still, I felt I had to add one little last word on the matter. Everything Steven outlined made sense. However, was there one last ditch possibility for the beacon's presence? Pilots could and did use radio transmission to navigate, but while radio beams could direct them, they could not pinpoint location. As in the sad case of the B24 *Lady Be Good*, pilots could over or undershoot. Could the beacon then be a visual aid to pilots flying on the radio signal in nasty weather with the code beacons to point them in the direction of the landing field a few miles north? It was not that the beacon was guiding pilots to a dangerous antennae field, but alerting them to the radio station, as anyone flying the east coast *could,* and in my opinion likely *did,* use the WBT-AM signal and beacon marker to determine position.

There was an ominous silence from Steven. I think I had finally exasperated him. I have a tendency to pick at a point till it bleeds.

 Steven finally wrote back after several days of silence. In that email, Steven included a document from 1970 which outlined the regulations for airways obstruction lighting. In essence, there was a need for standardization of airway obstruction lighting. It reiterated his contention that all airway rotating beacons should be clear and the WBT-AM beacon was most likely a hazard beacon.

Why was I so unwilling to accept that it had been a hazard warning? Warnings were critical to pilot safety, just as critical as lights marking the route for the airmail pioneers. Why was I fighting this point?

How many pilots might have crashed into the beautiful Blaw Knox tower had the warning red light of the beacon not flashed them away from it? This piece of history, so rare and so unique, might not still be standing like a sentinel of the past were that rotating beacon not there doing its duty.

Steven answered my flurry of emails, as I asked question after question, clarifying his conclusion. Finally, in what sounded like exasperation, he asked, *"Where are you going with all this discourse?"*

I answered, *"I am only trying to gather all the facts about beacons that I can. I wanted mostly to learn about the rebuild of the tower, and the biography of the wonderful young engineer who did so without plans! A side point is the mystery of the beacon. On the way to my attempts at understanding, I have learned a great deal about the airmail system, early navigation systems, WWII era flying and pilots, radio towers, engineering, tenacity of character, and the role of radio, however tangential in all that. It is amazing to me how starting with one thing of which I knew nothing, I could explore and learn about a whole wealth of things I never intended to explore, nor would have likely ever explored on my own. What a joy of discovery! Astounding how researching such a seemingly unimportant, unnoticed thing as a radio tower can harvest such a wealth of our country's history and past."*

I think at that moment, Steven felt the first real sense of camaraderie towards me. After all, he wrote articles and oversaw a website devoted to a short period in aviation that many people thought very little about, if they knew anything of it at all. He was at heart, a researcher and historian, and the history of the airmail beacons captured his heart as completely as the Blaw Knox towers and WBT-AM aircraft beacon had captured mine. I think perhaps with my last email, he saw a kindred spirit.

Later, he sent me an essay he wrote on Automatic Direction Finding. It helped clarify how early pilots relied on radio signals to navigate. It was so well written that I have reprinted it with his permission exactly as he wrote it. [See addendum]

The WWII *Lady Be Good* bomber that had supposedly overflown the radio station, should have known it had overflown, according to his essay. It would have had an ADF needle pointing at first to the front and then moving to point to the back when the pilot passed over the station he was homing on. I asked Steven how, given this information, the *Lady Be Good* had overshot her radio station target.

"There are lots of problems with the *Lady Be Good* story," he told me, "Stay tuned!"

I also remembered that John Eney, who had helped me explore the possibility of the beacon being an airmail beacon some months back, had theorized that the beacon was to help pilots homing on the station to have a visual cue when they flew over it so they didn't overshoot. I asked Steven what he thought of that.

"I don't think so," he said. He felt the demise of *Lady Be Good* was the result of "crappy navigating." The needle would have shown the pilot when he overshot the radio target. And by the way, Steven mentioned, that was true of any radio direction navigating. There would be no need for a visual cue of a beacon. The needle would go from the front to the back of the gauge. The pilot would know from that when he was over the station whose signal he was following.

A couple of weeks later, Jerry Dowd, the chief engineer of WBT-AM, sent me an email with pictures of the beacon, and a note. They were fantastic pictures, and I presume that meant he had gone on the roof. He said Crouse-Hinds had manufactured the beacon but there was no name plate with rotation rate or any other information. There were several surprises in the photographs. First, the beacon was open on only one end; the other end was closed. It was clearly red, not red and white. It had a glass, not Fresnel lens. It was pointed at a steeper angle than I had suspected. I sent the photo to my brother John, who had been assisting me in my research.

"The angle is around 15 degrees," John told me, "That would be consistent with an obstruction beacon, not an airways beacon. It would only be seen by planes very close to the station."

"Well," I said, "True...but it would also be seen then by pilots using ADF who needed a visual cue as they flew over the station."

Steven, as expected, disagreed. It was an off-the-shelf beacon, not an airways beacon at that angle, nor did it have a Fresnel lens which all airways beacons used. And don't forget...it was red, not clear. He insisted it would not be needed for ADF. It was an obstruction beacon, purchased from Crouse-Hinds, probably installed in 1937 when Red 7 was established. It had nothing to do with WWII, the Airmail route, or lost pilots. It was as ordinary as me.

WBT-AM Beacon - photo courtesy WBT-AM

CHAPTER TWENTY-ONE
A Towering Inspiration

I could not believe it. I looked in my rear view mirror and there was a rotating red light. It was not visions of the WBT-AM beacon. It was a cop. He had pulled me over because he noticed my inspection was overdue by a month and the registration expired as well. I never get tickets. I don't speed. I am courteous to policemen, and I abide with the spirit and letter of the law. And here was a cop, pulling me over for an expired inspection and unpaid registration!

He at least took pity on me, and told me if I took care of the inspection and brought the papers to the courthouse, the charges would most likely be expunged. My record would be clean again, and I could walk among humanity without hanging my head in shame. The ticket was issued in Concord, an hour from my house. Thus, I had to drive an hour to return to the scene of my crime with my now up to date documents in hand.

I headed off to Concord one fine morning, knowing it was best to deal with unpleasant tasks head on. I hated that ticket sitting on the counter, accusing me every time I walked past. It glowed with a malevolent cast and I could almost hear it cackle from the corner where it was stuffed amongst my pile of to-do lists. I grabbed the ticket and my new registration, and drove for an hour to the Concord Court house.

After being frisked and wanded so I could enter the court house with the other criminals, I slunk up to the third floor. I showed my documents, and a surprisingly kind receptionist told me all charges were removed, and I could go free. She smiled, and even winked as I took my documents back and asked, "Is that all? Am I free to go...no bail or anything?" I left her little window feeling liberated and even giddy. As I stepped onto the elevator, an old man with a badge and a walkie talkie in hand greeted me.

"Will it rain?" he asked.

"Oh, I don't think they are expecting rain, are they?" I answered.

"Tomorrow they are," he said.

"Oh that's right," I said, "I guess there *is* a hurricane churning in Florida. We might be getting the outer bands soon."

"Hurricane!" laughed the official, "I know what a *real* hurricane is!"

"Oh?" I said, "Did you live through a big one?"

"Camille," he said, "Back when I was in the military."

I learned that the friendly gentleman had been in the Air Force. Of course, this sparked my intense interest. He had been a pilot during the Viet Nam war, and afterward flew as a private pilot locally.

We stepped off the elevator. "Are you familiar with the WBT-AM radio towers?" I asked.

"Sure," he said, "As a private pilot I used to fly from Florida to Charlotte on the radio beam. Everyone did. Easiest way to navigate back then!"

I would've kissed him, but it might have been misconstrued, particularly inadvisable in the courthouse with all those armed guards around watching me and the other criminals.

Easiest way to fly to Charlotte was on the WBT-AM radio signal?? I asked him to repeat that again. I wanted to etch it on my arm with a pocket knife, but of course, was not allowed to bring my pocket knife into the Concord Courthouse.

"What about all your other navigational tools?" I asked.

"I could have used them, but it was just easier to tune into WBT-AM and home in on the station. Everyone flying into Charlotte did that. You know, it was a million watt station -- that beam stretched from South America to Canada."

"I know," I said, my grin stretching across the Atlantic, "I am researching those towers...and I am particularly interested in their role in navigation and WWII."

I fumbled in my purse for something to take notes on. I pulled out the ticket, that wonderful, glorious traffic ticket and flipped it over to the blank side.

"Did you know about the Delta Airbase on the east side of Charlotte?" he asked.

"No," I said, surprised. In all my research, I had never come across anything about the Delta Airbase.

"Well, the military during WWII used to ferry their planes to the Delta Airbase for maintenance. They came from all over the country to get parts, and train pilots. Then they would send them off overseas."

"Do you think it was possible those WWII pilots flew in on the WBT-AM radio beams too?"

"Not only possible, but probable," he said, smiling at me.

This was just getting better by the moment. I had goose bumps. I swiped at tears in my eyes. The policemen roaming the halls were beginning to watch me with their hands on their holsters. I guess I looked a little half crazed.

"You know those towers are rare and special," I said.

"I know," he said, "My aunt owned a home not 500 yards from them. I used to play in the shadow of those towers."

The incredible web of interlocking lives that were snapping in place on this journey I had begun made me shudder with delight. This wonderful angel of mercy was Jack Berry. He served in the air-force from 1968-1972. He gave me the name of his flight instructor who still lived in the area, telling me he would be able to give me more information about Delta Airbase.

Delta was now an airport salvage yard, still operative. The 2,000-foot single airstrip of the old airbase had not even been paved. It had been a small airport with very little information about its role in WWII on the internet. A brief blurb on Wikipedia noted that the Delta Airbase was formed by a Mississippi group in order to train and outfit pilots for WWII. (Charlotte Aircraft Corporation, Wikipedia). Paul Freeman, author of the website, *Little Known Airfields: North Carolina,* added that Delta Airbase, known initially as Grove Airbase, was established somewhere between 1941-42. His website displayed several aerial photos of the Airbase as well as anecdotal memories of old WWII planes and plane parts dotting the airfield. The airbase still exists today, but mostly as an airplane parts company. The airstrip, much smaller and being encroached upon by development, is still there. I had driven by that section of town many times, completely unaware of the presence of this piece of Charlotte's interesting history.

Jack Berry's flight instructor, Larry Morris, later agreed that pilots up and down the coast had used the WBT-AM signal. He urged me to contact Bob Beitel, an aviation historian. Bob was an infinite source of information, and talked with me at length. He had been an early pilot with Eastern airlines for 33 years. He concurred with both Larry and Jack regarding the use of AM radio stations to pilots, particularly back during the war days.

"Broadcast stations were very valuable back then to pilots," he told me, "Especially internationally. Back then, that was sometimes all they had! Now, flying on AM radio was not precise, but it would get you there. It was more powerful than the NDB (nondirectional radio beams) that were installed to help pilots navigate using ADF (automatic direction finder)."

"Do you know if WWII pilots trained at Delta Airbase?" I asked.

"No, I don't know that. I know they did at Morris Field, you know where Charlotte Douglas airport is now. In fact, it was a military facility back then. They had advanced training for pilots before they would be shipped overseas. But I don't know if Delta Airbase did. I am not sure how it got the name 'airbase'. I suppose it might have been an auxiliary training strip to Morris. I do know that in Columbia, SC, there was training for the B25 pilots. Back then, no airplane had ever taken off from an aircraft carrier. It was in Columbia that pilots were trained to do that. In fact, I am from the Lynchburg area, and one pilot training from Columbia flew in to the side of a mountain in Lynchburg. Navigation was not very good back then."

If they made it to Lynchburg from Columbia, then they flew right over WBT-AM. According to Jack Berry, flying on the AM radio beam of WBT-AM was the easiest way to head north.

"You know," continued Bob, "that training in Columbia, SC was part of what really turned the war around for us. Pilots learned how to navigate to take off and land on those aircraft carriers right there in Columbia."

Delta Airbase, just twenty miles or so from the WBT-AM towers had been used to train WWII pilots, who undoubtedly had been trained in ADF using the powerful WBT-AM radio beams. The pilots in flight school in Columbia had plausibly trained similarly. Given the archaic navigation systems of that time period, homing on AM radio beams, used even in the 1970s by Jack Berry and other pilots, would assuredly have been used by the pilots who had even less advanced navigation choices at their disposal than pilots of later years had. There was now little doubt that the WBT-AM towers had guided WWII pilots, either as part of their training, or on their journey north to Labrador and other bases en route across the Atlantic.

"Do you think those Columbia pilots were also trained in using ADF with AM radio stations?" I asked.

"Oh I would think so," said Bob, "Funny coincidence- just this week the FAA has issued a decree that all the ADF beacons are to be dismantled. They are very expensive to keep operating and with all our radar and GPS now, they feel they are no longer necessary. But you know, I have recommended to everyone I know not to remove the ADF from their aircraft. When emergencies occur and the other equipment fails, you can use broadcast radio beams to home in using ADF. I flew all the way to South America and could hear WBT-AM! And I would fly all the way back home on that signal!"

I asked him how a pilot would know when he was approaching the target radio station. My long suffering expert Steven had told me many times that pilots paid attention to where the needle pointed to know if the station was before them or behind him. But he also mentioned an interesting point. There were two sensors with the ADF, and one controlled where the needle pointed. Sometimes that sensor malfunctioned.

Bob explained that the skillful pilot could actually turn the plane, turn down the radio volume, and listen carefully to the signal. If the signal got stronger, the station was on the side where the plane was turned, and the pilot could know which direction the station lay.

Steven had told me a similar story in his explanation of Amelia Earhart's disappearance. He thought it likely the trailing antennae had been left behind. Obviously,

ADF was not perfect but problems could be compensated for, as Bob had explained. Earhart was truly out of luck over the ocean with no strong AM radio signals, nor visual cues to help her. *No visual cues.* This thought sparked another question.

"As a pilot," I asked Bob, "What do you imagine would be the use of a beacon at WBT-AM atop the transmitter building?"

"Well, if it was marked on the navigation charts, it helped them know when they were passing WBT-AM," he said, "And of course, alerted them to the antennae field."

It *was* on the navigational charts. The beacon had *perhaps* mostly warned of the towers. I was willing to concede this point in light of its dual role. It was first and foremost, (*possibly*), an obstruction beacon. But secondarily, it had alerted the pilots that the station whose signal they had been homing on was right below them.

Bob told me that Charlotte was key in overseas training of WWII pilots. His understanding was they had already received basic training at bases all over the country, and when they were ready for final advanced work, they went to Charlotte. And they flew from the south, in all likelihood, homing on the powerful, widely used, and well known WBT-AM signal. They probably listened to the Briar-hoppers, the hillbilly group that entertained WBT-AM fans since 1934, as they flew those long miles over a dark country with black-out conditions. They would sight the rotating red beacon, and know they were directly over WBT-AM. Those brave new pilots would then veer slightly West to

Morris Field (now Charlotte-Douglas) or east to Delta Airbase, some to train, and some to repair and outfit planes before heading to the front. And some would likely have passed over a little boy playing in the shadow of those three diamond shaped towers, who would one day follow their signal across the skies himself.

*****

Declassified documents from the Army Air Force crinkled in my hands. I held copies of lcttcrs from 1944 describing the function of Delta Air base during the war. The Air Force Historical Research Agency had written from Maxwell Air Force Base in Alabama. They had discovered that the Delta Airbase was not used in USAAF training; however, they had found a small document that shed some light on Delta's role in WWII. It was used during the war for the overhaul of Lycoming aircraft engines under contract of Warner Robins Air Service Command, Ga. The AAF archivist, Archie DiFante, found that the primary Air Force Base in Charlotte, Morris Field, which later became the Douglas municipal airport, did operate a combat crew training station. Pilots were trained in light bombardment at that facility, but Delta was not assigned to Morris Field.

Delta Air base was already a civilian Aircraft Engine Shop when the Army found it. The Army Air Force poured some $20,000 into the base to increase staff, expand the facility, and outfit it for the Army Air Force engine overhaul work. It was set up to overhaul the Lycoming R680 Engine.

Delta airbase was small, but the engines they repaired were critical. The Lycoming R680 engine was the first light aircraft engine the Lycoming Company built and was very successful. Interestingly, Lycoming started off with sewing machine engines. Wise. Start small where engine failure doesn't endanger anything more important than a skirt. In 1907, Lycoming began producing car engines and moved into aircraft engines in the 1930s.

The 'aviation Bible', *Jane's All the World's Aircraft 1942,* reported that during the years of 1941-2, Lycoming dedicated its entire R680 engine production to the war effort. The engine was used in a variety of aircraft that was critical in WWII, including Avco, Boeing, Curtis, Cessna, Beechcraft, Stinson, and Spartan airplanes.

Sadly, Delta Airbase had faded into obscurity but they had clearly played their part in the war. They had not been wildly successful in their foray into contract military work. The quota of engines, at least in April 1944, was less than half of what the AAF had contracted for, judging from the weekly output. Problems with location, transportation, and communication all beset the little airbase. Still, the few engines they repaired had a small part in our ultimate war superiority during WWII. They certainly serviced a diverse and important variety of war aircraft. Little known and unremembered Delta Airbase, like the under-appreciated Blaw Knox towers, had played its part in the war effort, and then slowly evaporated from notice. Even the current owner of the land knew almost nothing about Delta's history. But it was highly likely that the pilots flying in for repairs had followed the path of the well-known WBT-AM signal.

*****

In a fortuitous volunteer stint at a nearby nursing home, I was introduced to two WWII navigators. Both were intelligent and still mentally sharp. I instantly arranged interviews, hoping to find the needle in the haystack -- the pilot who had navigated on WBT-AM beams.

The first, Joe Wheeler was born in Greenville, Mississippi on August 6, 1924. He was stationed in Okinawa as a radio operator with the 6th Emergency Rescue Squadron.

"Our job was to find pilots who were lost, and try to bring them back. Anyway, I flew in a B17. We had a boat attached to the bottom. We called it the 'Flying Dutchman'. If a pilot went down in the water, our job was to find him and if need be, drop the Flying Dutchman to pick him up.

"Our group was responsible for the air defense of China. When the bombers took off to China, the fighters would take off first to clear the way. And then we would take off after the bombers, circle near, and if any pilots had to ditch, we would be there to drop the Flying Dutchman.

"One day, we were coming back from China. Being Radio Operator, I could listen to all the channels. In fact, I could pick up AM radio stations as well."

"From the United States?" I asked, my ears perked.

"Oh yes, all the time. In fact on one of my trips I heard on an AM station that FDR had died. I was the one that told my crew the president had died and I heard it on the radio while flying! I had great equipment. I could hear lots of radio stations."

"Did you ever use AM stations to navigate?"

"Well we could! We were trained so that if we had to, the pilot could home in on a radio signal, then find another one, and then triangulate his position. We did that all the time in training. I would listen for radio stations then plot our position. The navigator always knew where we were going, but I could tell you exactly where we were by listening to those AM radio stations."

"Did you ever do that when you were lost?" I asked.

"Well, I could have, but we never really got lost."

"Did you ever find your way back on radio signals?" I asked.

"No," he said.

As usual, I tried forty ways of asking the same question. He *could* fly on radio waves, but in his war experience, did not. I moved on to my next victim.

*****

Robert Dychus, the second veteran, was sitting in the hallway in his motorized wheelchair. He had just finished listening to the entertainment for the afternoon, a cellist playing old time music. Bob followed me into the front parlor, and we sat by the window.

Bob was the first person in the Pacific Theatre, if not the whole war, to use radar in the Military. It was a good thing he knew how to use his knowledge. It saved thirteen lives even before he reached his base overseas.

Bob was born April 26, 1922. He served in the Air Force from 1942 till 1945. That fact alone was one fraught with irony. The Air Force initially turned him away. In the end, the Air Force begged him to train with them. As a young adult, 19-years old, Bob wanted to be a pilot. He tried to enlist with the Air Force. He was given a battery of tests and passed all but one. Bob weighed 139 pounds, but the air-force minimum weight was 150.

"How about this," Bob told the Air Force, "I'll go home and be back in two weeks and I will gain 11 pounds."

So Bob went home and ate everything he could get his hands on -- bananas, pork, bread, cakes, creamy milk, butter, steaks, potatoes. He had no scale, of course, at home. No one during that time period did. In two weeks, he returned to be weighed. He tipped the scale at exactly 139 pounds.

"You didn't gain a thing!?" I cried.

"Not an ounce," he laughed, "So I went home and waited to be drafted. I worked a year in D.C. and then got drafted into the army. They gave me all their tests and at first told me I would be joining the first infantry. Well I wasn't happy about that, but I figured I had to go. Then after all my tests, they called me back in and told me the Air Force wanted me because I had done so well! So off to Biloxi, Mississippi for training. When I finished six weeks of basic training, they gave me more tests. They told me they wanted me to go to a school in Chicago. They wanted me to learn radio maintenance and operation. A year later, they told me I'd done so well that they wanted to send me to Boca Raton, Florida for training in radar."

"Radar!" I exclaimed, "That was brand new technology back then!"

"Sure was," said Bob, "It had never been used in a combat situation. Ever. I was on the very first plane that ever used radar in the military. Anyway, it was a one-year course. When we finished, they shipped me to Norfolk to be ready to head overseas. There was a crew of twelve men who were flying to Foggia, Italy, and they had room for one passenger...me. So we took off from Norfolk. The plane had some trouble first at Boston, Massachusetts. There was very bad communication, and we were never told we were flying right into a terrible thunderstorm. It got so bad that at one point, the plane dropped a thousand feet in seconds. That was mighty frightening. But we got through that and landed in Newfoundland.

"Newfoundland was the stepping stone to heading off to the North Atlantic. We spent the night, and then had an 11-12 hour flight the next day to the Azores, a group of islands in the Atlantic where we would refuel before going on to Africa. Well, we flew about eleven hours, and I noticed the crew was getting real excited. I asked them finally what was going on. It turns out that they couldn't find the islands."

"Did the navigator try to home in on an AM radio?" I asked hopefully.

"No...I don't even know if the Azores had a radio station," said Bob, "But even if it did, they were forbidden to use the radio. The Germans would have found us if we used the radio. So we were lost, and we were running out of gas. I told them, 'Let me speak to the pilot. I have radar.' Now they had never heard of radar. No one had heard of radar! 'What's radar?' they asked. 'With radar, you can see in clouds or at night,' I explained, and I tried to explain to them what radar was. They refused. They told me my radar would use their precious fuel. I begged them. After some time, and still no sight of the Azores, they were desperate. Finally they told me, 'OK, use this radar.'

"So, I turned it on, tuned it in, and all of a sudden, I saw a picture sixty miles to the left. I told the pilot, 'I see land. I don't know if it is the Azores...though I don't know what else is out here so I think it must be.' So I told him it was on the left and he had passed it by 20 or 30 miles. I told him to make a hard turn, and keep turning, till we were pointed straight for it. 'You're getting close!' I yelled, 'Hold it straight now!' That went on for about fifteen minutes and then he shouted, "There they are! I see the islands!' So we landed safely and refueled. I asked him, 'How much fuel did we have left?' 'Ten-minutes worth,' he told me. We had ten minutes of gas left."

If it had been the wrong island, there would have been no gas to refuel and the likelihood small of being found and rescued.

While stationed in Africa, Bob heard the word 'television' for the first time. A fellow soldier mentioned it after Bob showed him the miracle of radar. Bob gleefully recounted the story that led to his lifetime career after the war.

"'What's television?' I asked him. 'It's radio with pictures,' he said. I paused, and stepped back. I felt like I'd been hit. I actually prayed a little bit. Remember, I had learned a lot about radios, I had even applied for a job in radio before joining the service. I thanked him then, and told him now I knew what I was supposed to do with the rest of my life. 'I will work the rest of my life in Television.' "

And guess where he applied and got his break in both radio and television engineering? WBT-AM! Here was the WWII navigator who once was lost over the Atlantic. And while not quite as I had initially envisioned, he *had* in a sense found his way home on the WBT-AM signal. But the WBT-AM signal was not all that had drawn him. A greater Signal apparently accomplished that.

Bob ended up working his entire career at WBT-AM, though mostly working in television, not radio. He remembered the towers, and mentioned their miraculous range. He could not recall the beacon, however. He did recollect in detail the meeting that was arranged with the chief engineer at the time, Mr. Minor, who hired him on the spot. He spoke of his lifetime of work at WBT-AM with towering passion, feeling God had arranged how his life's career would unfold. He knew how special the station had been, and that the signal from those diamond towers was nothing short of miraculous.

CHAPTER TWENTY-TWO
A Towering Passion

Maybe the miraculous was possible. What could it hurt to find out? After Tony arranged the meeting with the special woman, he flew out to New York and spent the evening on his job. He checked out of the hotel in the morning and took the train to Sara's house. She loved her brother and had been eagerly anticipating his meeting Sanya. While she tried to down-play expectations, she herself was filled with expectation. In her eyes, they were perfect for each other. She had arranged a lavish day. Tony arrived to see a stretched white limousine in Sara's driveway.

"What's this?" He asked.

"Our chariot awaits," Sara said.

"But no pressure," laughed Tony, feeling a bit like Cinderella as he dipped into the limo.

The limousine turned into Sanya's neighborhood.

"She lives here!" asked Tony, startled, "I have been running by this place for years! It's on my favorite running route when I visit." Sara just smiled.

Sara's husband, Scott, and Tony went together to knock on Sanya's door. The dark-haired 'special' woman answered the summons. She embraced Scott, while Tony stood back, all the while staring at her. He hoped he wasn't gawking too obviously.

"Tony, this is Sanya," said Scott.

He grasped her outstretched hand, and for a foolish moment thought, "I am in love."

Sanya was born in Sarajevo, Bosnia. She had led an idyllic life in a beautiful country, worked hard and received her degree in dentistry. She immigrated to the United States in 1988. When Sanya left her beautiful country, it was the gorgeous, peaceful land the world embraced during the 1984 Olympics. However, by 1990, Sanya's mother and father were still in Sarajevo when concerns that war was inevitable were growing.

"Bring your brother to America," her father asked her, "Now, while you can. I could not bear to have him pulled into this war."

So Sanya immediately brought her brother to America. Meanwhile, Sanya's parents remained behind, grateful their children were safe but increasingly worried for their own safety. Finally, with deep foreboding, Sanya's father told her mother to pack only a few things, wear only black and they were to leave immediately. They concocted a story of going to attend a funeral. They went through four different barricades in their escape to Serbian territory, and during the tense moments of questioning, repeated the story of a funeral they must attend.

The very next day, after their feet touched safely in Serbian territory, the Bosnian border was closed. It would remain closed for several years. Sanya's father always believed that if they hadn't left when they did, they would have been killed, as many of his friends were in the coming months. Within a few months, Sanya was able to bring her parents to the United States.

Sanya had met an American man while skiing in Sarajevo the year before leaving Bosnia, and they married when she settled in the United States. She applied to dentistry schools. Her degree from Bosnia would not allow her to practice in the USA.

Sanya was a determined and confident young woman. She did not bemoan this set back but applied to several schools. Despite having already worked for five years for her degree in Sarajevo, she would be required to take an additional three years of courses in the United States. That is until Temple University not only accepted her, but developed a whole new program to accommodate the brilliant young woman. If she passed the boards, which she did, she was allowed to enter as a sophomore, cutting her school requirements by a year.

"That taught me something very important about America," Sanya told me, "I learned this was a country where everything was possible."

She began her successful practice as a dentist in New Jersey. She had two daughters, then after eighteen years of marriage, divorced. It had been difficult. No divorce is ever easy, but she had survived, moved on, and then thrived. She was content. A great job, great daughters, great home. She needed nothing more and had long ago resolved that she would perhaps remain single.

She had been in a relationship after the divorce, for many years but was not happy. The relationship was fun, but she was not in love. Like Tony, she had not been sure love was really possible anymore after all the disappointment and hurt.

But this man, thought Sanya, as she settled across from him in the limousine. This Tony might be different. He was certainly handsome, confident, respectful, and considerate.

When he spoke to her, he touched her knee, and animatedly embarked on a story with guileless candor. His comfort in his own skin made the often awkward first moments of meeting someone melt away. She gazed at him, and thought, "This man *is* different." Tony peered at her and felt like he was seeing the picture he had formed in his mind for years of the woman he knew was not out there, but had created in his heart, building her in his dreams.

Sara had stocked the limo with champagne and wine, and the happy group drank a toast to life. Sanya watched Tony, and marveled at his gentle ease with his sister, his gentlemanly treatment of her. She forgot she had just met him. It felt like she had always known him.

They had brunch in a wonderful restaurant in the Italian section of town. The limo driver waited patiently, and when they emerged from their spectacular meal, they were driven to the Union League. As they wandered around the Union League, Sanya reached for Tony's arm. She nestled her hand in the crook of his arm, laughing and leaning against him, as though he were her oldest friend. It felt strangely as if he were.

As they walked through a door, he gently placed his hand on her lower back, and Sanya felt as though an electric shock had leaped across her spine.

"It was magnetic," she said, "I had never experienced that pull before with anyone."

They returned to the limo, where the driver smiled and asked where they would like to go now. He noticed the sparks electrifying the air around the handsome couple. He was happy for them, these kind and beautiful customers. They directed him to Barnes Foundation, where a magnificent, priceless collection of art was housed. Tony and Sanya wandered happily in the rooms, her arm still resting in his, and she told him she especially loved the paintings of mothers and their children. She pointed to one that she particularly liked.

They exited the museum through a small gift shop. Tony vanished, and the other three waited for him outside the exit. He appeared a moment later with a canvas print of the painting that Sanya had most liked. She accepted the gift, incredulous.

"For me?"

"I know you liked the painting," said Tony, grinning.

Sara and Scott walked in front of the new couple. Sara was smiling, and imperceptibly nodding.

"And now?" asked the limo driver, opening the door to the happy group.

Next stop was a party at the home of a doctor friend of Sara and Scott. The doctor lived a good distance across town. Tony and Sanya exchanged stories in the limo, and as they talked, they leaned towards each other, his hand resting on her knee.

The doctor's home was almost as impressive as the Barnes Foundation. Millions of dollars worth of exquisite art adorned the walls of the mansion. The buffet spread for guests at the party was as impressive as the art.

"Oh, the chocolate lava cake!" exclaimed Sanya.

Tony, remembering the limo driver, took a plate of the chocolate lava cake and crept outside.

"For me?" laughed the driver.

"I appreciate you driving us," said Tony, ever cognizant of those who work hard and are experts in their fields, trying to make a living just like he was.

"It was a day filled with art, food, drink, and love!" Sanya reminisced later.

The long and glorious day drew to a close and the satiated group sat in the limo as the driver was directed to return to Sanya's house. Scott and Sara sat contentedly snuggled together as the limo slowed in the moonlight, and halted.

Tony opened the door and then reached his hand out to help Sanya from their magical carriage. He put his hand on her back and walked her to her door, feeling the first slight tinge of nervousness.

He would be respectful, though his heart longed to hold her near and not let go. Instead, he kissed her chastely on the cheek and turned, walking a bit reluctantly back to the limo. Sanya watched him move away and wondered if it was possible she was in love so soon.

Tony turned back, wondering about the wistful look on her beautiful face. He returned to her and hugged her, feeling that maybe love was real; maybe what he had thought was impossible was possible after all. She turned her face towards him and kissed him. In America, everything is possible!

Over lunch, Sanya had mentioned that she would be in Miami in two weeks. As Tony forced himself away from the front step, he was already contemplating how he could rearrange his busy schedule. How could he be in Miami in two weeks? He would find a way. There was a tower he could work on in Miami in two weeks...

Tony did not quite dare to believe it, after all he had been through and lost in love. She is the woman of my dreams, he thought, returning to the limousine. He had been so certain true love really could not exist. It had not existed for him. Never had he felt so certain that he had finally found what he had always wanted, at least while standing on the ground.

*****

Jerry Dowd, chief engineer at WBT-AM returned to his desk, his mind filled with the myriad duties of a radio broadcast engineer for a top tier radio station. He loved his work, but there were never enough hours in the day.

As he sat down, he noticed a folder that was unfamiliar to him. He opened the folder and data logs, photographs, and archival information fell onto his desk.

"What is this?" he asked himself. As he thumbed through the material, he thought of the writer, the one that had incessantly bugged him about the beacon on the transmitter building. There were pictures from the 1930s through the 60s and information about that very beacon.

Jerry stood up and walked over to his co-worker, the one certainly responsible for the archival folder.

"Where did you find this?" he asked.

"What is it?"

"Photos, data from the '30s...didn't you put it on my desk?"

"No Jerry, I have no idea what that is."

Where had it come from? Jerry asked several suspects, but no one knew how or why that folder had appeared on his desk. To this day, Jerry has no idea who placed it there.

Puzzled, Jerry sat down again. Two old photos showed the same shot of the transmitter building. The first one, from 1945 showed the open wire feeders to the massive tower array that had been in use before the coax wires of today. He peered closely at the roof. No beacon! There was a guard shack, and he remembered that that had been erected during WWII. The station was considered a target, so armed guards had been stationed atop the transmitter building. But no beacon!

Next he looked at a photo from 1963. The guard shack had been removed by then, but the open wire feeders were still in use. He remembered reports of how labor intensive the open wire feeder system had been -- required constant maintenance. There, in the photo, on the roof was the beacon! It had a clear lens. He shook his head, feeling a little sorry for the writer, despite her somewhat annoying persistence.

Before looking at the other documents he found her address and sent her an email, attaching the photos:

I would not get real excited over the red light on the WBT-AM transmitter building roof.

We recently discovered these pictures. It was NOT there for WWII. If you look closely at the 1945 open wire photo (before we had today's coax) you see the WWII GUARD SHACK on the roof. And NO LIGHT. The guard shack was real; we did have military guards during a portion of WWII, as did most High Power radio stations, when there was concern of a takeover of a broadcast station by the enemy. If you look at the 1963 picture, you clearly see a CLEAR lens in the light. The light was apparently added as a CLEAR spot light to help the engineering work at NIGHT on the massive WB1-AM array and old open wire feeders (that required a lot of maintenance). At some point the clear lens was broken and they apparently had a spare red lens. Sorry the story is not more exciting.

Jerry Dowd

CHAPTER TWENTY-THREE
A Towering Validation

A month before that crushing email from Jerry, I was noodling around Facebook, when one of the pictures stopped me. It looked like a view from a tower, or perhaps a fighter jet. The picture was posted by one of my Facebook acquaintances. I wasn't even sure how I knew him, but he had posted a few things that had to do with veterans.

"What is this picture of?" I asked.

"A fighter jet," he responded.

"Are you a pilot?" I wrote.

"No," he said, "I was seated behind the pilot."

"Were you a navigator?"

"No, but my great uncle was. He flew in WWII."

I stared at my computer screen.

"Did he ever fly on radio beams?" I asked.

"Let me ask him and get back to you. He is 93 and sharp as a tack."

A few moments later, my Facebook friend wrote back, "He says he did, and he has lots more to tell you. He says you are welcome to call."

The next day, I called James R. Critchett, the 93-year-old WWII navigator. It took me a while to track him down. At age 93, he is still driving, and had been out and about all day. When he called me back at 5:00, he had just returned home. His voice was clear and vibrant, his hearing apparently unimpaired, and he was smart and eloquent.

"You sound great!" I told him, "What's your secret?"

"I have no secrets. I love the outdoors. Fresh air, I guess."

I wrote "fresh air" on my notebook and circled it.

I told him the nature of my research about the role of the WBT-AM radio towers and the beacon as potential navigation aids to WWII-era pilots.

"Well we did do that," said James, "We flew on the beam all the time. If you were flying on the beam, you would hear a hum, and just as you flew over the station, you would hit a dead spot."

"Might that be why the beacon was at the WBT-AM site, to alert pilots that they were flying over the station?"

"Yes, that, and to warn pilots of the tower height."

"But the beacon isn't on the tower," I said.

"It's not?"

"It's on the much lower transmission building roof," I said, "Do you know why that would be?"

"Well we used beacons all the time to help alert us to landmarks. I used to draw radio facility charts. I would show the direction of the airways, you know the beam for navigational purposes. I would show all the towers, all the beacons."

With mounting excitement, I told him about the Red 7 airways and the position of the WBT-AM beacon right at the outer edge of where the airways jogged north.

"Why do you think it was there?" I asked.

"Well it certainly could have been there to warn pilots to turn north to follow the airways. Of course I don't know that for sure, but it makes sense. They would also have sent up a code so the pilot knew what station he was passing over."

I was confused. I knew the rotating beacon didn't flash a code. Then it dawned on me that perhaps something else sent the code.

"Are you talking about the rotating beacon, or code beacons on the towers?"

"Code beacons on the towers. As the pilot flew over, those beacons flashed a code. The pilot knew exactly what station the code was for, so he knew exactly where he was."

"There *were* code beacons!" I cried, "They are mentioned on a 1937 sectional, but then not mentioned again. Why would they not be mentioned in later publications?"

"For security purposes, without a doubt," James said.

"Can you explain? Do you mean when WWII came, the beacons were no longer flashing the code so they wouldn't let the enemy know where they were?"

"Yes, exactly. Things were crazy then. The Germans were bombing boats right off the coast. We knew they could come ashore. I am quite sure the code beacons were shut down so the enemy wouldn't know what station it was. And so they wouldn't know the direction of the signal from the towers. Anything we could do to decrease their ability to navigate. I feel very confident the code beacons and the rotating beacon were used to aid navigation, and the code beacons would have been shut down during the war for security."

Everything James said fit my research. The code beacons were not obstruction beacons -- they were navigational beacons, used to tell pilots what radio station they were passing over. Pilots would also know that the beam was north/south. When the war came, the code beacons were extinguished, almost certainly at the government's behest so that no navigational information would be provided to the enemy. And without the code beacons, perhaps the rotating beacon was even more critical in helping our pilots know what to look for to identify that they were passing over Charlotte, NC, specifically over WBT-AM where the Red 7 airways jogged north.

"James, if you were lost over the Atlantic, would you look for AM radio signals to get back to shore?"

"Well you could, but AM radio signals are not very strong and do you know how many of them there are? You would have to know what frequency to tune in to."

"But how about back then, when there were a lot fewer stations, and only a handful of really powerful ones. Could you have found the strongest signal like WBT-AM would have produced, and then flown to shore on the beam?"

"Yes," he said, "And if you could find the signal and you were lost, you would most certainly want to do that."

"So it is possible a lost WWII pilot found his way home on my towers' signals?" I asked.

"It is," he said.

"Did *you* ever get lost?" I asked.

"Never! The radar was very good."

"But you think it is possible pilots *did* get lost over the Atlantic and find their way home on radio beams, maybe even WBT-AM beams?"

"I think it is *probable*," he said, "But there aren't many of us left anymore. It would be pretty hard to find him."

It was enough for me knowing he was *probably* out there, or had been. I could almost picture the relief on the lost pilot's face as he soared over the diamond towers, with the beacon blazing the light that told him he was safely home.

*****

I read the disappointing beacon update email from Jerry Dowd with mixed feelings. I was grateful he seemed to be warming to me, but saddened by his conclusion. Despite so many pilots telling me otherwise, including the conversation I had just had with James, was the beacon really now not even as glorious as an obstruction beacon? Seriously? It was not WWII vintage, not glamorous in any way, used in the pedestrian role of a work light? I thanked Jerry immediately, and told him while he *seemed* to have solved our mystery, would he indulge me in some questions? Why would a rotating beacon be used for work site lighting? That really made no sense. A steady beam searchlight would be much more logical for that purpose. And also, I had historical documents that claimed the beacon *was* there in 1937. How could it not be on the roof in the 1945 picture? And certainly, the beacon looked like a WWII-era beacon. Was it really manufactured in the 60s?

Jerry wrote back instantly, a kind letter, sensing my disappointment. He said history is filled with errors when one is counting on memory. He related a story of when he moved into his new house eight years ago, and then later had to verify some things for the insurance adjuster, he had to find all the documents. He couldn't even accurately remember what happened within the past decade. No wonder the facts were fuzzy on the beacon.

I told him the strange thing was that this was not a memory of the beacon being there in 1937-- it was a document *from* 1937. It was a Dept. of Commerce sectional map used by pilots and it clearly stated there was a rotating red beacon and two code lights at the WBT-AM site.

"Fascinating. May I see it?"

After my email, Jerry must have been bitten by the detective bug and had discovered yet another interesting fact in the mysterious folder.

He found a manual for an old work light, manually operated, clear lens, made in 1950 by Graybar electric. Other documents indicated it was installed on the old guard shack and used as a work light for the array. The guard shack, and work light were removed sometime before 1970. The clear beacon was not the rotating beacon after all.

The next day, I saw another email from my new friend, Jerry Dowd. The subject line said, "Teaser." I

Bulb inside beacon, labeled Airways
Beacon - Photo Jerry Dowd

eagerly opened it.

"Roofer had a ladder today. Opened beacon because I could reach it. Has two bulbs. They also

move side to side. More pics on disk when I get it complete. No indication it was ever white or red. So no need to ask any questions yet. I don't know!"

The picture of the bulb inside the beacon was labeled "airway beacon." It was not an obstruction beacon. It was an *airway beacon!* Then a flurry of pictures came from Jerry. One was of an identification plate. The lettering was a little worn. It said either DCR or DCP,

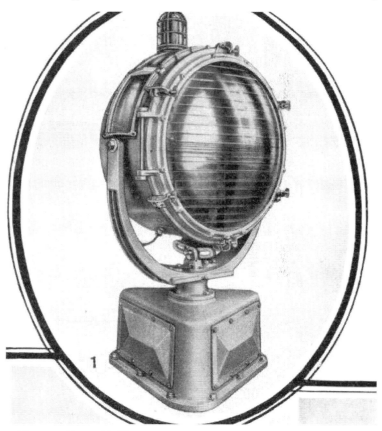

Picture of 1931 DCB 24 inch airways beacon made by Crouse Hinds

followed by the numbers 42118 and on a new line 1000 T. The 1000 was the wattage of the bulb. What could the letters be? I googled the letters hoping to chance upon an answer. Nothing. Returning to the picture, I peered more closely. Could it be a B? DCB. The first hit on my search engine when I googled DCB was an article about air mail beacons, of which the DCB 24 was the type placed every ten miles to provide a lighted path for the pilots. DCB stands for Directional Code Beacon. 24 referred to the size -- 24 inch lens. It had a picture and description that matched our beacon exactly.

Jerry's pictures kept coming. Next he emailed me a picture of the complex and automatic spare bulb changer from inside the beacon. The photo looked just like the picture from the article I had just read about DCB 24-inch beacons. This intriguing device allowed quick and automatic changes of the bulb should it burn out. At the base of the changer was a small identifying plate. It had a catalogue number and was also made by Crouse Hinds. He continued to remind me he had no answers, so don't ask.

I sent the photos to my old beacon expert friend, Steven Wolff, and to my brother.

"Is this an airways beacon?" I asked them.

Meanwhile, Agent Jerry Dowd had found his own article about airmail beacons as well as a detailed picture of a DCB 24. He noted it looked exactly like our beacon, even down to the two screw holes on the top. In the picture, a small light sat atop the beacon. Our beacon didn't have the light, but it had the screw holes for the light in exactly the correct position. Interestingly, the description of the 1000-watt airmail beacon noted they had parabolic mirrors to reflect the light, not Fresnel lens! Our beacon had a shiny parabolic mirror inside.

By now, Steven Wolff had responded. He conceded it was indeed an airway beacon, but felt that it was not an airmail beacon. He said it was non-directional, not on an airways, and had the airport code light on top (or at least the capacity for one.) His guess was that it was an airport beacon.

This is odd. What would an airport beacon be doing at WBT-AM, which has no landing field?

While mulling over this dilemma, Crouse Hinds wrote back to my email asking for any verification regarding our beacon probably made in the 1930s. Their entire Airport Lighting Division and Obstruction lighting experts had been going back and forth on my beacon, and were not able to identify it. It was nothing like any of their airport beacons. If even the manufacturer could not identify the beacon, what hope did I have of doing so? And if I needed replacement parts, they suggested I contact radio equipment repair shops.

Jerry had read over old log entries beginning in the 1930s, searching for entries about the beacon. He now suspected, based on log entries that the beacon was on the roof from at least 1937 (when it was also first mentioned in the Dept. of Commerce documents) until now. The log entries depicted regular maintenance (indicative of easy access to the beacon -- e.g. on roof, not tower) which stopped suddenly in 1962. Why? Bulbs were changed often, suggesting heavy, ongoing usage. This was not a beacon for special events, like those announcing the opening of a new car sales lot. It appeared to be used daily.

Long ago, I had found documentation of another airways beacon in Charlotte, this one officially commissioned and atop the historic North Carolina National Bank building. I had even tried to find it unsuccessfully on a drive downtown. That beacon was decommissioned in 1977. Jerry noted a tantalizing tidbit -- the bank beacon was commissioned in 1962, the very year that entries in the WBT-AM logs about the roof "rotating" beacon ended.

Jerry hypothesized that whatever entity controlled the airways beacons had switched the role of airways beacon for the area from WBT-AM to the bank in 1962. The bank was taller, the beacon more modern, and more visible than the WBT-AM roof. In 1977, the bank beacon was shut down due to the presence of so many taller skyscrapers around it, blotting its effectiveness.

"Why wasn't the WBT-AM beacon ever licensed, as far as we can tell?" I asked.

"I'm not sure we have been looking in the right places," said Jerry, "It may have been an informal agreement to help out, like we still have with FEMA, and with the government during the Cuban Missile crisis. Or it could be all our records were transferred to the Bank Building."

I found the current management agency for the old NCNB building, now the Tryon Building, and called them. Surprisingly, they had never heard of the beacon, nor had the maintenance men ever noticed it. The bank building had changed management groups many times, however, and our best guess was it had been removed when decommissioned in 1977. I wondered if the name plate, screwed on the base of the beacon, with the label DCB 42118 (or possibly 42113) was the license number. I was increasingly convinced it perhaps was licensed but the records were indeed lost.

Jerry offered to contact the FAA in Atlanta, to see if he could track down any information about when the beacon, or even, *if* the beacon was licensed.

In the meantime, he found more photos of the original tower right after a cyclone hit it and took down the top portion in 1941. There was no wreckage of a rotating beacon, but there *was* wreckage of a flashing fixed beacon. Thus, the 1937 documentation of the 24 inch rotating beacon had to refer to the beacon on the roof.

"I will contact the FAA for good luck," said Jerry, "However, I have more documentation on the WBT-AM coffee pot than I have on this beacon!"

The FAA had nothing to add, and thus, we were left with strong suspicions, but no certain answer. Sometimes, we have to move on with *near* but not *absolute* certainty. It is much like faith in that respect.

It appeared that my early speculations about the beacon had indeed been correct, but we may never know for sure this side of Heaven. The beacon was turned on by 1937 (possibly before, but at least according to air charts up to 1937, there is no mention of it) and was always on the roof (which explains the frequent log entries and apparently easy maintenance from the 1930s-60s). It was an airways beacon and useful at WBT-AM since WBT-AM was one of the south's powerhouse stations, a prime station for ADF

(Automatic direction flying). It also was only a few miles from two different airports, and indirectly useful in the war in guiding the planes that chugged in for maintenance at the little Delta Air Base only a few miles northeast. It was directly situated at the northward jog of the Red 7 airways and also for the common north-south air travel route used by the first major regional airline, Eastern. It was either on or very near the spur to Charlotte of the CAM 19 (airmail route). The tower had its own flashing beacon, thus the airways beacon was not an obstruction beacon, (too low and redundant), but a beacon to guide and alert land position as pilots overflew the well known WBT-AM station.

At one time there were code lights, but they were likely on the tower. The code lights either flashed the station code as a landmark, or perhaps directed pilots to the landing field at Delta or Douglas Airport. In 1962, the FAA changed the official airways beacon to the NCNB building in downtown Charlotte with a newer beacon, and taller roof. At that point, log entries of the WBT-AM beacon maintenance end, and presumably, it was no longer used from that time on. The light had shown on earth for a time, and guided many, but then vanished, leaving only the clues that it had once been brilliant, now a conundrum of illumination and mystery.

An amazing story, if true, and it smelled true to me.

*****

Tony clutched Sanya's hands as she opened the door of her friend's house in Miami.

"I can't believe you are here!" she said, amazed, "How can this be true!?"

"I have something for you," he told her, handing her a small box.

She smiled at him, and took the gift. "What is this, Tony?"

"Open it," he said.

She lifted the top off the box and saw a bracelet. It was the bracelet Tony had bought months ago in Spain for a "special someone" he was yet to meet. And now, he had met her. Somehow her presence had illuminated his heart long before he knew she was there, a light from the past now glowing in his present like a beacon.

*****

I gathered my documents about the beacon all together to put them away, when I glanced again at the chart of the airmail beacons and the Charlotte spur with three beacons pictured. Two were labeled, C1 and C2. The third was not numbered but was at the Municipal airport. That map had been from 1937. When I had first looked at the map, I had not known for sure that the WBT-AM Beacon was an airways beacon. Nor had I known that the early airmail beacons looked like the WBT-AM beacon.

Who might know something that I had not yet uncovered?

"I assume you have already contacted the Charlotte Aviation Museum?" wrote Jerry Dowd.

"Before or after I read that question on your email?" I asked the condemning air around me. I quickly found the number for the Charlotte Aviation Museum, and after a few questions, was directed to Richard

Lautensleger, a volunteer with the Charlotte Aviation Museum Library. He asked if I wanted to come by, bring the map and my documents and he would see what he could uncover.

Richard was waiting for me outside the building when I arrived. He was a tall, thin man, now retired from his career as a pilot flying private planes. He loved flying and loved history, thus spent Thursdays each week volunteering at the library. He ushered me in to a small building crammed from floor to ceiling with books, most picturing airplanes on their covers and bindings. The place smelled of old books. Model airplanes dangled from the ceiling, and framed prints of old airplanes dotted the walls. There were four men in the building. All but one appeared to be of retirement age.

I had hit the jackpot with these gentlemen. Not many folks venture into the Aviation Library. While the volunteers kept busy cataloguing and putting things away, I could tell that my presence was appreciated.

"No one cares about history anymore," said Claude, one of the librarians, "We have all this wonderful information and everyone is too busy playing video games to come in and see it!"

"And," added Bob, a WWII veteran, "the folks that can tell them about the past are dying."

I explained my project and asked if they could identify the beacon positions on my map. Had there been historic airports that might have coincided with C1 and C2? I assumed Douglas Airport was the municipal airport shown due west of Charlotte.

Over the next two hours, all four men flooded me with maps, photos, and books. I was particularly interested in their knowledge of old, little known area airports. I had only the day before discovered that the very first airport in Charlotte, called Charlotte Airport, and then Cannon Airport had had the first official airmail delivery in the Charlotte area on April 1, 1930.

"Did it have a beacon?" I asked.

They didn't know, but immediately went scouring through their archives and then came back with an ancient photograph of a mother and her child in front of an airplane. The Cannon airport building was behind her, and peeking over the roof was a tower, just like all the airmail beacon towers I had seen with what certainly looked like an airmail beacon atop it.

"Folks," I said excitedly, "I think we just found C2."

Next, they managed to uncover an old picture of Douglas Airport from 1938. It also had a tower with a beacon on top. That was in all likelihood the municipal airport beacon depicted between C1 and C2.

The map was not to scale, and it was very hard to discern exactly where C1 was located. It appeared to be about ten miles southwest of downtown Charlotte.

"This looks about where the WBT-AM towers are," said Richard, "But it is hard to say. There are no airfields that I know about that were anywhere near there in 1937. Maybe it is the beacon at the towers?"

Maybe, I thought smiling. Just maybe. However, intellectual honesty compels me to admit that C1 was more likely in the Gaston county area. Later, I discovered that a concrete arrow marking an airmail beacon as well as the tower base remains on Kings

Pinnacle in Crowder Mountain State Park. This was almost certainly the airmail beacon marked on my map as C1. Since the map indicated only 3 airmail beacons were in the CAM 19 spur, I had proven that WBT-AM was not an airmail beacon. However, it was exciting to have found where those three airmail beacons *had* been so long ago.

Important as the airmail routes had been in the development of aviation and navigation, little is known about them today. Huge concrete arrows, like the one on Kings Pinnacle still cross the continent, the last remains of that amazing period in early flight history.

Sadly, almost none of the towers and beacons remain. Almost all of them had been dismantled long ago. I understood the despair of the librarians as memories of the past grew dim. They watched me leave clutching the photos of the airmail beacons, and eagerly asked me to return soon.

Cannon Airport 1931, beacon visible over right hangar roof. Photo courtesy Charlotte Aviation Museum Library

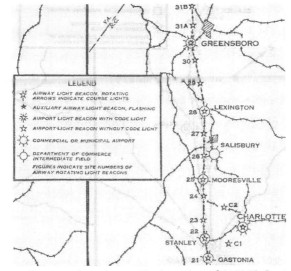

Map of beacon placement on Charlotte Spur of CAM 19. Dept. of Commerce, 1937

Charlotte Douglas airport, 1938. Postcard courtesy of Charlotte Aviation Museum Library

CHAPTER TWENTY-FOUR

A Towering Conclusion

So why the diamond design? The beacon mystery was solved. That pilots could and likely *did* find their way home on the WBT-AM signals had been corroborated. My mission was almost complete. Now, why had Blaw Knox ever construed this unusual tower design?

Triangles are the strongest structural shape. A diamond is two triangles lashed together. Perhaps strength was part of the rationale. However, with four faces, it was more easily collapsed than a tripod, thus stability was compromised.

Secondly, the design incorporated elements of both a self standing and a guyed tower. The geometry of the design allowed the diamond tower to stand secure with a single set of guy wires. Presumably, that would be less draining on the radiating capacity than the zillions of guy wires necessary on the skinny towers, but also allowed them to be built to greater heights than the self standing towers. Thirdly, those Blaw Knox towers had a tremendous range. It certainly *seemed* they were a superior design in terms of output, though there had been no proof of that. And fourthly, the diamond is forever. Both the Nashville WSM Blaw Knox tower and the WBT-AM towers are among the oldest remaining transmission towers in the world.

"Why hasn't anyone just done a comparative computer model?" I asked my brother. I suppose someone may have. I had not come across one, but that didn't mean it wasn't out there.

"Well back when they were designed," John told me, "They just didn't have the computer capability to do so."

"But we have computers *now* that can do it," I countered.

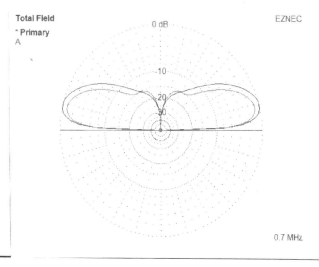

John Ceccherelli's comparative model of radiating strength of Blaw Knox and uniform width antenna, the Blaw Knox being the outer trace.

"Yes," said John, "But the only people who care generally don't have the training of hard core RF engineers."

"But you do," I told him.

"Yes. I will send you the model soon."

His model proved what we had suspected from the start. He had produced a graph comparing the radiated signal strength of a uniform width and Blaw Knox tower. The towers were in the middle of the plot. He told me to think of it as if looking at a landscape photo. The inner line was the skinny tower, the outer line was the diamond tower. The difference between the two was about 2dB (decibels). While this was not a striking advantage of the diamond tower over a skinny one, it did shed light on why the original Blaw Knox engineers *may* have favored the cantilevered tower. The diamond Blaw Knox towers were better signal transmitters. Not a lot better, but better nonetheless. And they were indeed, *pretty*.

However, what I noticed immediately was that the shape of the transmission plot was roughly a heart. How fitting that the proof of the tower designer's intent was in the shape of a heart! No one *really* cared about the minuscule difference between various tower transmission capabilities outside of a small elite group of radio engineers. Not many people seemed to notice or care about these old towers, why they were built, whether they were pretty or not, or even that only a few of them remained scattered on distant corners of the earth. No one seemed to be concerned that a vintage beacon had an unexplained role, and unknown origin. The old are often forgotten with the encroachment of the new.

I really never expected to develop an affinity for an inanimate hunk of metal. Who would envision that studying a radio tower would end up revealing passion, drive, dedication, patriotism, talent, tenacity, courage, innovation, and love?

I had come to know and admire the man who picked up the pieces left in a hurricane's wake, and recreated perfectly what had been destroyed. I learned the stories of many brave men who had stood on this earth even a little longer than the towers had, many whose stories had never been told. They, like the towers, were growing old. One day, their message would be extinguished, and the value of their experience might drift away like dust. The blueprint of their lives would disappear. We might never understand exactly why they had been here, and what the purpose had been for their brief moment in eternity, what unique roles they had played, what special wisdom of their years they had to impart.

As one by one the old WWII pilots blinked and then vanished, the towers would still be standing. At least I hoped they would, those diamond towers with a message shaped like a heart, blinking on my horizon.

*****

Tony and Sanya rendezvoused in Las Vegas while Tony was attending a Broadcast convention there. He took her to "The Top of the World", a revolving restaurant high above the glitter of Vegas. As the sun cast golden and magenta rays that reflected off the glass of a thousand windows below them, he took her hand and gazed into her dark eyes.

The muted light shone on her hair, dancing like living threads of fire. They had only been dating for a few weeks at this point but he was as certain of his love for her as he had been certain that he could rebuild the fallen Blaw Knox towers. He reached for her hand, and she reached back with a slender arm, so elegant and lovely. The world slowly spun beneath them; the distant towers he had worked on speckled across the horizon.

Tony surveying perfectly rebuilt tower
– courtesy Ted Bryan estate

"I'm all in," he told her.

"Me too," she laughed, "I'm all in, too."

Tony, the man who climbed so far above the earth, was now at the highest point of his life. And he thought he had gone as high as he could go, dangling above the horizon on a 2,000-foot tower! Now, he thought, *now* I know what it *really* is to be on top of the world. The man who had miraculously rebuilt the broken tower, now miraculously rebuilt his broken heart. Out of the richness of God's abundance, yet one more blessing flowed.

*****

It was 11 p.m., and Tony was preparing to leave for work. He had bounded out of bed, having napped briefly, giddy with excitement. He glanced at his phone before leaving the hotel; saw that he had missed a text from Starr. She was finishing her finals and would be meeting him the following week. She sounded happy, he thought, gladness rising. Finals were going well, and she was proud of her grades thus far. "Can't wait to see you Thursday!" she wrote.

She would spend a few days with him in Columbia, visit with friends, and see her mother. Then for Christmas, Tony's extended family along with Starr would be gathering in Cancun. Tony would take a week off, and spend the vacation surrounded by his beloved relatives on balmy beaches, speaking the language he had first known in which he'd first heard the whispers of love.

There would be no building on this vacation, not even a sand castle. He would sit on the shaded verandah, looking out over the aquamarine waters, and listen contentedly to the chatter of his brother, sisters, and mother. He would shade his eyes, and watch his precious Starr stretching her toes along the surf line with her cousins, upturning shells.

After that vacation, Starr would be leaving immediately for Spain, for a semester of study abroad. She had high hopes for that semester. She hoped to come home with a potential husband. And then she would return to Spain forever. Tony smiled as he read the text, telling him when she would arrive in

Columbia. He thanked God again for the blessing of his daughter, this shining star he loved so well.

Other stars twinkled in the sky as he gathered his gear duffle bag, where his safety harness was carefully stowed. He felt like it was already Christmas morning and he was about to open the best gift of all. *I am the luckiest man alive,* he thought. He stretched and noticed his muscles ached. He had done a brutal training ride the day before -- miles and miles on his carbon fiber bicycle with its thin tires. He had pushed himself, but he always pushed himself. He challenged himself each time he set off on the beloved Cannondale, going faster each time, improving, building muscle, building endurance -- *building, building, building...*

He had set the alarm just in case, but it was unnecessary. He could not wait to head off to work, while the rest of the world was settling down snoring. He was wide awake, joyful with anticipation of his work that day. It had been one of the busiest months of his life. He was a little overwhelmed with all the work, but he wasn't complaining. He knew that to have more work than one could handle was a blessing, especially in this economy. He had never been without work, he thought briefly. Perhaps there had been disappointments in life, but it was hard to remember them. His heart was full of the joys. There was little room for anything else.

He dressed warmly. It was bitter cold outside but he knew he would not even notice the cold once he started up the tower. He would notice the rumble of the city, the lights sparkling above and below, the familiar cadence of hook, climb, hook. Even in the bitter cold he would begin to sweat as he scaled the tower. Of course, after an hour or two, the wind would begin to seep through the layers. Then he would feel it. After the four hour shift, he would be numb from the cold if he didn't dress properly. He grabbed an extra shirt, after flipping on the weather channel. Was it a three or four layer night?

He stretched again and looked out the hotel window before leaving. A stop light blinked red below him, and a single taxi-cab pulled away from the curb. Broadway and 6th were both within sight. Normally, in the day, both avenues were throbbing with people. Now, only a handful scattered in the wind. Straight across from his hotel he could see the enormous skyscraper. The three tiers were lit up, the tower itself too high and setback for anyone from the ground to see at this vantage point.

The world is just going to bed and I am about to start my day, he laughed. His mind was already thinking over the duties of the day, and then the calls he needed to make the following day; the other tower jobs he needed to manage. He would be sure to stop by the hotel fitness room after a quick nap, get in a workout, and dissipate the lactic acid that he felt in his thighs. Only the most impossibly overfull days kept him from that routine. Or perhaps he would sleep a few hours, and then take a run across town, along the Hudson into lower Manhattan and back. Then he would shower and tackle work calls. He might sleep before the next evening on the tower, or he might not. It would be a busy day, but first, the tower waited against the black sky, its multicolored lit tiers beckoning him.

Tony left the hotel and decided today he would walk along Broadway to the tower. Where throngs of people had gathered at tables along storefronts during the day, homeless people now shivered. Some slept, some gazed with blank expressions, the frosty air laying a barely perceptible sheen of white on their hair. Tony stopped to place some money in one man's cup, though the man didn't stir or acknowledge the offering. The streets were quiet, almost eerie with the indigenous poor creeping out in their tattered coats, and soiled jeans. Policemen strolled by but mostly left the homeless people alone. In the day, the cops might be more likely to herd them along, and they would creep desolately to their corners and alleys.

Tony knew that when he retraced his steps the next morning, the scene would be quite different. Now the sky was darkening around the city, folding in upon itself in relative repose. In the early morning, as he came off the tower, he would see the kiosk covers being unlocked, the bagels being stocked alongside the pastries, the newspapers being carefully lined up beside the magazines. There would be the jingling of keys and locks, the snapping of tablecloths, and awnings, the murmuring of workers, many complaining about the bitter cold. As the sun began to send tentative rays in the frozen air, the homeless people would melt away. The tables would slowly empty. The sound of traffic would gradually growl in a growing cacophony of brakes squealing, horns blaring, and tires rumbling. The streets would slowly awaken; one by one people beginning to scurry along the sidewalks, men in dark coats with shoulders hunched and hands clenched deep in their pockets. But for now, the city was laying its electric spirit down for the night, and while not quite a hush, it was subdued and peaceful.

As Tony entered the building, a familiar security guard waved to him. He went through the routine, emptying his pockets, and placing the gear duffle through the security scan. The procedure went quickly, no one else from the crew yet arrived. That was another advantage of working while the owls swept the alleyways for mice, and the bats flickered among the light posts -- one was nearly alone, and there were no crowds to battle. The city never completely slept, but it was resting. That was the only time he could work on this tower. All other times of the day, it was busy broadcasting. For these few hours, its hum would be stilled and the tower builder would climb higher than perhaps anyone on earth at that moment.

He retrieved his belongings, smiled and waved to the guard and punched in the elevator button that would take him to the highest floor. He had a special clearance card that allowed him to rise above the level where others would have to disembark. When the elevator disgorged him, high above the earth, he stepped out and headed to the room where he and the inspection team would gather. Just through the door to the roof, the tower was perched.

Slowly the other crew members arrived. As always, they first discussed the bitter cold, how heavy the wind gusts were, and how many layers of clothes they should put on. It was always a guessing game. Once on the tower, they had only four hours to work. They would not want to take the time to come down to add clothes.

If one overdressed, and grew too hot climbing, it would be uncomfortable, and when the sweat cooled as he paused to inspect an area, the cold would permeate like an icy bathtub filling around him. If he underdressed, and was cold from the get-go, the four hours would be numbing misery.

"It's a two-layer day, at least," said Jim.

"I don't know," said Joey, "Last time you suggested two layers it took me three days to thaw my knees enough to bend."

"Fine, three layers," Jim amended.

"I'll see your three layers and raise you one," shouted Scotty.

Tony laughed and with the others, unzipped the gear duffle. He pulled out the heavy safety harness. They talked about Christmas plans, the holidays, and the week on the tower before them.

"You going anywhere special?" asked Bill.

"Meeting my family in Cancun," Tony answered.

"Rough life," he said.

"I'm the luckiest man alive," agreed Tony.

"So three layers?" asked the last worker, Terry.

The banter continued and the six men settled on three layers. It was easier to cool down than to warm up, it was decided. Tony reviewed the level they would be inspecting and pointed out the areas he wanted them to pay particular attention to. Towers require on-going regular inspections for a variety of reasons -- to check the equipment's condition, inspect for areas of stress or metal corrosion, examine connections. In a city with such harsh winters and high winds, as well as the corrosive effect of the nearby salt-water ocean, careful, regular visual inspections were critical in maintaining the tower's structural integrity.

"Gear up?" asked Joey.

Tony glanced at his watch. It was now almost 1 a.m. They'd consulted with the Radio Frequency engineer, then pulled on their clear goggles, and three layers of clothes. The safety considerations had been reviewed. The power had been shut down and it was time to get to work. The men snapped on their safety gear and filed out onto the roof. The banter died down. Tony always steeled himself to focus. He never forgot that his work would be highly dangerous if he lost focus. With much to do in just a four-hour window of time, the men immediately took their positions at the tower base.

Tony paused and looked out over the roof edge. The city lights sparkled like jewels in a dragon's lair for miles and miles around him. The air was frigid, the stars crystalline in the dry, breezy night. Traffic never stopped in this city, though he was so high up that its individual sounds melded to a steady roar. The tiny cars below looked like ants. He listened to the rumble of the city, the indistinct tumult of the city's heart beating nearly 1,450 feet below him. The regular high pitched whine of a siren pierced the rumble, a shriek rising to the clouds, tapping against his ear drum with the ever-present wind.

No matter how many times he stepped onto this roof, he was struck by the beauty, the similarities, and the changes. The intensity of the noises of the city was still present, a half mile in the air, but all garbled together so that it rose with a dull hummmmmm... As far as he could see were lights, but now, where the moon had not so long ago reflected upon ripples of water, there was the luminescent blue white of ice on a distant ice skating rink. Lights crisscrossed all over the city, but for one dark rectangle where the immense Central Park lay. In the distance, he could see the Statue of Liberty, and the Brooklyn Bridge. Puffs of clouds floated by beneath him.

Tony on Empire State Building Tower - courtesy Tony Fonseca

"I am above the clouds," he thought.

Tony uncapped the lens cover from his camera and stepped to the edge of the roof. Just one picture, and then he would begin. He was gripped with a sudden gasp of awareness that he, Tony Fonseca, stood high above one of the most magnificent cities on earth, on one of the most iconic buildings ever made, working on one of the most coveted towers any tower engineer could long for. The Empire State Building Tower! He, Tony Fonseca, just a plain man, working on the most famous tower in the world! Looking out over sights millions would pay to see, he was exhilarated and humbled. It never got old, this searing realization of how far he had come.

Me, he thought, for the thousandth time, *Look where I am! Oh if only my dad could have seen this, seen me here.* He framed in his view finder the photo that would remind him of this piece of heaven he had the pleasure of entering.

"I am the luckiest man alive," he thought again, snapping the panoramic photo of the city slumbering beneath him. The crew was already beginning to scale the tower. The magical moment was broken by the task before him. Like the others, he could not imagine living with two feet planted always on the ground.

Later, he would send me a photo of that moment with the text, "How do you like the view from my field office?"

"It is colder than my ex-wife!" shouted Scotty, his words snatched by the wind.

"Nothing is that cold," said Terry.

Once, Tony had brought Starr up to the observatory deck, where she could see the tower structure. She was a young adult by then. She had never shown much interest in his tower work. It was always Skylar who asked Tony for details about what he did. But she had wanted to see *this* tower. And her father had arranged it. She looked up high at the tower base and then stood and looked out over his world. For perhaps the first time, Starr realized how dangerous his work was. It was magnificently beautiful, and she knew also why he loved what he did. But she felt fear for the first time that this dizzying height, hanging to that thread of a spire, could harm her "querido padre". She had never been afraid of heights, but standing so high, the city spread far below, the tower rising still higher into the stratosphere, she felt a stab of worry.

There was little talk now. They were all seasoned tower veterans. No one but the best would be on this tower, this pinnacle of a career. They knew what they had to do, and each one of them was an expert in his particular area. The crew climbed higher, pausing to inspect a beam. Tony watched. The angle was perfect for a photograph from this vantage point, the night so dark and vibrant with stars struggling to pierce the glow of the magnificent city. And then he thought, "Focus", snapped on his lanyard, and began to climb.

*****

Sanya had a picture of what would be the perfect engagement ring, but hadn't shown it to Tony. She knew they would likely marry one day, but she would not presume. Sara, Tony's sister, saw the photograph and sent it to Tony.

Too late. Tony had been plotting the engagement for months. He had already been to the jewelers and bought the ring that he hoped his beloved would cherish. The picture Sara sent him looked nothing like the ring he had chosen. Tony was not worried. He felt certain that what had poured out of his heart would be what Sanya would most want. He had given her no hints about his plans, nor asked her anything about ring shopping. He wanted the proposal to be a complete surprise.

Afraid to leave the beautiful ring when he travelled, he carried it with him in his pocket. In the hotel, he kept it in the safe. He worried he would lose it but he wanted to insure that Sanya might not chance upon it by accident. He carried the ring wherever he went, while drafting the perfect proposal. This most important day in his life must be flawless, and he meticulously drew the blueprints of the day in his mind.

First he thought he would ask her to marry him on Christmas Day. Christmas was such a magical, special, beautiful time. He was so grateful to God for the gift of Sanya. How fitting to propose on the birthday of Christ! The ring jostled in his pocket, and he thought he could not possibly wait till Christmas.

Well then, he would ask her to marry him on Thanksgiving. He prepared the speech in his mind, thinking about how thankful he was for Sanya. How fitting to propose on the day we celebrate thankfulness! The ring jostled in his pocket, and he thought he could not possibly wait till Thanksgiving.

Sanya and Tony went to the observation deck of the Empire State Building in late October. Tony pointed to the tower so high above the city, where he had just finished installing the electrical system for a spectacular light show set to music on October 31st. They had watched the glorious light show together, and Tony was proud of his work that had flashed across the skies of the best city on earth while seated beside this wonderful woman. The ring shifted in his pocket, and he thought, "I should ask her now, right here. On top of the world. She makes me feel I am on top of the world!"

But no. He had wanted to ask her in a beautiful place as the sun set and had already arranged a trip to Key

West for her birthday, November 7th. He would stick to the plan. He would wait, though he didn't know how!

Finally the day arrived. He arranged for a trip to Sunset Key from their hotel in Key West. They would take a boat to the little island. Tony called the restaurant maître d' and begged him for the best table they had to view the sunset.

"It is the best day of my life," he told him, "Please give us the best table!" The restaurant was booked, but the maître d' promised that for Tony's special day, a special table would be secured.

As they waited for the cab to take them to the dock, Sanya had no inkling of Tony's intentions for the day. She saw the three gifts in Tony's hand, and was thinking to herself she was the luckiest woman alive. Such an extravagant and romantic birthday celebration!

The time for the cab to arrive came and went. Tony nervously looked at his watch. The boat was leaving soon! They would not make it. Frantic, he went to the concierge and begged for help, "What can I do! I can't be late! This is so important! This will ruin all my plans!" The concierge, glancing at Sanya and sensing the panic (and perhaps the source) in the poor man's pleas offered to drive the couple to the dock in his own car. Tony and Sanya gratefully leaped into his car and they raced to the dock.

"You cannot get on the boat," said the dock manager, as they hurried from the car, "They are ready to leave and pulling up the boarding plank now."

Tony grabbed Sanya's hand and they ran to the boarding ramp. The workers paused and unhooked the rope, ushering them through. As soon as the couple boarded the boat, the ramp was pulled away and the boat churned off to Sunset Key.

Tony and Sanya were led to a table at the far edge of the restaurant, closest to the ocean which reflected the magenta reds, fuchsia pinks, and blazing ochres of the setting sun. Tony smiled gratefully at the hostess. It could not have been a lovelier spot to watch the sunset and tighten the final bolt of a dream he'd been building for a lifetime.

Tony clasped Sanya's hands, and said, "Would you like your gifts now or later?"

(Please now, now, now!)

"Oh now, of course!" laughed Sanya.

She opened the first one that Tony handed her. Shimmering diamond earrings.

"Tony, I love these!" She instantly removed the earrings she wore and put on the sparkling new ones.

"Here's your next gift," he said.

It was a glorious bracelet, which she instantly clasped onto her wrist. The setting sun glistened and danced on the waves, to the tune of the surf. The light sparkled on her new earrings and bracelet as she playfully struck a pose.

"I have one more little gift," said Tony, "It isn't much but I hope you like it."

He handed Sanya the third gift, his heart pounding. She carefully ripped away the wrapping paper and slowly opened the ring box. As she lifted the cover, a tiny light flickered on, a little beacon blazing its beam across the diamond.

Tony dropped to one knee, "Will you be mine forever, will you be mine forever...will you be mine forever..."

He was so excited he could not finish the sentence at first, then dropped onto both knees and gripping her hands, cried, "Will you be my wife forever?"

Sanya threw her arms around Tony, "Yes! Yes!"

*****

Back at work, Sanya could not always wear her ring while working with patients. She brought the little box with her everywhere she went. She thought she almost liked the box as much as the ring. She opened it, and smiled at the tiny beacon illuminating the diamond that signified so much, and thought of her future husband who at that moment was climbing another tower.

CHAPTER TWENTY-FIVE
Towering Discovery
April 1991

Ted Bryan locked the gates to the transmitter field, but then turned and looked again at the towers. He had been on the field looking over various readings in the tower building, making sure all was well. The station was humming away again, fully operational. No more complaints from Omaha. Just congratulations that the powerhouse of the southeast was completely back in business. An airplane flew overhead, en route to Charlotte-Douglas Airport. It dipped a wing and veered north. Ted watched it for a moment, the silver wings cutting across the vast expanse of deep blue sky high above the towers.

Now, he dropped his eyes and gazed at the three transmitters lined up like soldiers, with a stab of love and delight. What a rare wonder to see them intact again, standing in a stately row. How he had missed their lovely profile on his horizon! How glad he was to see them, his old friends, faithfully sending their message across such a broad expanse. The beautiful diamond Blaw Knox towers. How blessed he was to have had the honor of working on them so many years, and overseeing their rebuilding when all had seemed lost.

Tony, that young engineer, had been right. Had he not known which towers had come down, he would not be able to tell by looking at them now. The fresh red and white paint sparkled in the sun, resplendent against the sky.

The hawk that had visited every day of the rebuild was gone. He apparently liked what he saw, and having overseen the project, felt he could safely leave them now. When the final piece of the antenna was lowered, connectors firmly clamped in place, and the painting completed, the ever-present hawk had screeched, lifted into the sky, and disappeared.

Ted never saw the hawk again.

He glanced up at the beacon on the transmitter building. It reflected the searing sunlight, bouncing the rays back to the heavens. He had the blueprints from Tony Fonseca in his hand. Several copies had been made, and now he would place one copy in the transmitter building. The others were in the main office. He would place this copy in a long wide map drawer where it would be safe, and easily retrieved if needed.

"Let's hope we never need it," thought Ted, as he unlocked the door into the low brick building. He thought about what an incredible thing that young engineer had accomplished. To have recreated so perfectly those unusual towers, manufactured so many unique parts, and then present him with such a perfect drawing. It was nothing short of miraculous. There had been moments when Ted himself wondered if it could be done. The tower engineer had never seemed to doubt. How much easier the whole process would have been if they had had the original blueprints! Easier perhaps, but maybe the hand of God is more evident in accomplishing the difficult.

He pulled open the map drawer and felt it catch a little.

"That's odd," he thought. He pulled again, and saw the edge of a roll of paper was caught deep in the inner edge of the drawer. He carefully slid a finger over the edge that was stuck on the inner wall, and slowly extracted a large roll of old, yellowed plans.

Carefully, Ted cleared a nearby table and laid the roll on the clean surface. He slowly unfurled the document, knowing even before it was open what it was.

With a chuckle, Ted smoothed his hand over the original blueprints of the WBT-AM Blaw Knox Towers.

CHAPTER TWENTY-SIX
A Towering Epilogue
(the rest of the story)

I received the sad news in an email from Jerry Dowd, "Thought you should know Ted Bryan passed away last week." I was so sorry to hear this, but glad he had seen the rough draft of my book before he died. He had known he was to be immortalized in prose.

I tracked down the email of his son, Charlie Aldredge. I sent Charlie my condolences, telling him his father had been a wonderful man who had given unselfishly of his time and was the impetus to a book I was writing about the WBT-AM towers. In fact, I told him, "Your father is in the book! I will send you a copy when it is published." I thought that would be soon. The book was finished and in the edit process.

Charlie wrote back and told me he would be coming to Charlotte a month hence to clean out Ted's house. He said few people knew that Ted had an extensive historic radio collection. He also said he had found four carousels of slides. They showed a tower, knocked down by a storm.

"May I see those?!" I cried excitedly, "Those are of the rebuild of the Blaw Knox tower!"

"Not only may you see them, you may have them," offered Charlie magnanimously, "And you are invited to the open house when I come to Charlotte. I notified a whole bunch of radio buffs as well as the WBT-AM friends."

I eagerly accepted both the slides and the invitation. Just the week before, I had asked if WBT-AM had any photos of the rebuild. Jerry Dowd said they didn't. Tony had some, but couldn't find them. What a miracle that Ted had them, and his son understood that I would want them.

The day arrived, a hot sunny day. I almost cancelled, coming off a two week bout with the flu. I was not feeling fantastic, still a little wobbly on my feet. However, in the end, I decided I ought to go. I was very anxious to get the slides. During the process of writing the book, I had only envisioned the rebuild in my mind. There are a few pictures of the toppled towers on the internet, but I had seen none of the rebuilding. What a miracle and blessing that Ted had them hidden away in his amazing collection of old radios and broadcast equipment. I was honored and touched that Charlie wanted me to have them.

When I arrived, the back gate was open and a group of men were gathered around an open garage filled with vintage radios. I squeezed through the gate. As I approached, they turned to say hello collectively.

"Which one is Charlie?" I asked one gentleman. He pointed to a man in the garage deep in conversation with another radio enthusiast. He had the same kind and gentle expression I remembered of Ted, his father.

The gentleman introduced himself and asked if I belonged to the radio club.

"No," I said, "I'm a writer. I wrote a book about the WBT-AM towers."

Another man glanced over and approached. "Are you Vicky?" he asked.

"Yes."

"Hello!" he said, extending a hand, "I'm Bob White. Charlie told me about your book."

I was stunned. *Bob White*?! The man who had almost been crushed by the WBT-AM Tower crashing down during Hurricane Hugo? *That* Bob White!? I had assumed since Bob White had retired as chief engineer at WBT-AM before Ted became chief engineer that Bob was at the least, a very old man. Since no one had suggested I speak with him over all the years I'd worked on the book, I just assumed he was dead. I did not expect a man that looked approximately my age, alive and well.

"You are *in* my book! I thought you were dead!" I blurted.

"No," he laughed, "I am very much alive."

"How did you get interested in writing about the WBT-AM towers?" asked another.

"Well," I said, "My brother, a radio engineer told me about them, and Ted took me on a tour of them. That is how I knew Ted. But then, I wanted to solve all the mysteries that no one knew the answers to." I smiled at Bob, knowing he would understand.

"What mysteries?" asked another.

"Well first of all, no one knows why the towers are designed the way they are designed, the diamond shape," I said.

"*I* know," said Bob. I squinted in his direction.

"And what else?" asked another man. I snatched my eyes back into my skull, and turned from Bob to answer.

"Well there is a mysterious beacon on the transmitter building and no one knows why it is there or who put it there."

"*I* know," said Bob.

"You do?" I asked. He nodded.

"Well no one else knows," I said, "Believe me I asked. Ted didn't know either. Nor Jerry. Nor the WBT-AM historian."

"No, they wouldn't," said Bob, "But I was quite young when I hired on in '79. I met the people who were there almost from the start. I was beginning my career. They were ending theirs. I talked with them. They are all gone now, of course, as in dead."

"We need to talk," I said.

So Bob and I went into the living room, surrounded by Ted Bryan's old radio collection and WBT-AM memorabilia. Charlie sat on the couch listening.

"So, the beacon?" I asked, almost afraid to hear the answer.

"It was installed as part of the Federal lighting system for the airways," he said. I felt the hair on my arms raise.

"Why was it red?"

"They were color-coded, depending on the airways they were on."

"As in RED-7?" I asked, smiling.

"I don't know the name of it or where it went, but that sounds right. In fact they used to log when planes would pass overhead. When planes took off from the airport, they would look for the WBT-AM beacon; it was the first one by the airport and once they reached it, they would be able to see the next red beacon."

"Do you know where the next one was?" I asked.

"No, I don't. But the WBT-AM beacon was definitely installed for the airways system."

"Was it ever on a tower?" I asked.

"No, it was always on the roof."

"My experts told me an airways beacon would never be on a low building like that."

"That was on purpose!" laughed Bob, "If it were any higher, it would've interfered with the transmitter signal. The roof was the perfect place for it!"

"I was also told the angle, at 15 degrees was too high to be an airways beacon."

"No, it was just right for the planes passing overhead to know they were at WBT-AM and also for the planes leaving the airport."

Charlie was leaning forward, listening with rapt attention. "This is fascinating!" he said, "I am a pilot."

"Yes, so am I," said Bob.

We all talked about ADF, and flying on the WBT-AM radio signal. Both had done it many times, and agreed it was the easiest way to fly.

"But here is the curious thing," I told Bob, "If the beacon was installed for the Federal Airways system, why was it never licensed? As far as we can tell, it was never registered with the Air Commerce department, and there is no official record of it being installed."

"Well I knew the guys who installed it, and they told me that is why they installed it. But I am not surprised it was never licensed. They used to do a lot of secret deals with the government back then. And they didn't always go by the book. For example, you know the guys who started the station, Fred Laxton and Earl Gluck stole the radio tubes from Marconi in NY that they used to begin WBT-AM? They hid it under their coats while riding on the train! And the government was always interested in WBT-AM, did a lot of clandestine operations."

"Like when they took over the station to broadcast propaganda during the Cuban missile crisis?"

"Yes that, and did you know the FBI uncovered a plot to bomb the station?"

"I didn't!" I cried.

"Yep," said Bob, "So many stories I could tell you! So it doesn't surprise me at all that the beacon was never officially licensed. There were many 'unholy alliances' that went on behind the scene."

"And the tower design? Why the diamond design."

"It was pretty," he said.

"That's it?!" I cried, "Now I can't believe that! Engineers build for function!"

Charlie, a civil engineer himself, piped up now, "Not if an architect gets in the way!"

"Really," said Bob, "The design is not the most stable. A self standing triangle would be the most sturdy design. The original records are lost, but I think they just thought it was pretty."

Later, I asked Bob about one of my theories regarding the guy wires on the Blaw Knox tower. The unusual design allowed the tower to stand with only four guy wires.

"Would the guy wires affect the transmission? And if so would it make sense that less guy wires would be a better design? I mean the skinny towers have guys coming off them all the way up," I proposed.

"I never thought of that," agreed Bob, "You may be onto something. Guys do not disappear electrically, even with the insulators. The strongest radiation is theoretically at the center of that rectangular section, by the way."

"That is even more interesting," I said, "Most of the other Blaw Knox towers I saw have the guy wires right at the center...which presumably would not be the best place for them if they interfere electrically. But the WBT-AM towers, with their almost impossible range are guyed below center, at the base of the rectangular section. Does that design make sense in terms of optimizing transmission?"

Bob smiled at me and nodded.

I remembered how when I started this journey, my brother and I both felt that the decision to rebuild rather than replace was odd. It didn't seem to make sense economically, even with the equipment engineering study that would be necessary with new uniform width towers. We had always wondered if it was an emotional, not completely rational choice. I had asked Ted on that summer day eight years ago when I first saw the towers, "Did you rebuild because someone *loved* those towers?" Ted had told me that they would have had to reconfigure all their equipment if they replaced with "skinny" towers. He had intimated it was the fiscally sound choice to rebuild the Blaw Knox towers.

"Bob," I said, "You made the decision to rebuild, rather than replace...Why?"

"Oh gosh," he said, shaking his head with a wistful, reverent look, "Those Blaw Knox! We couldn't lose the Blaw Knox! Man, I loved them!"

Bob White - photo by Vicky Kaseorg

*****

Bob and I met in the transmitter building with Jerry Dowd. Jerry had collected several boxes of artifacts, logs and documents from the earliest years of the station and brought them out for us to look over. Slowly, Bob and I began to pore through them. I found a log from 1928 through 1929. I knew the beacon likely wasn't mentioned until 1937 which was the year I felt virtually certain it had been installed. Then I found the log from 1937! Entries began in September. I was fairly sure the beacon was installed in 1937, and I hoped not before September. Disappointingly, the first entry about the beacon was on Jan. 5, 1938. It noted that new bulbs

297

were placed in the "revolving beacon" to replace defective old ones. Clearly it had already been installed for some time.

"Any idea where the log book from 1936-1937 is?" I asked Jerry. He had no idea. It had vanished. Proof positive of who installed the beacon and whether it was ever licensed was apparently gone. However, entries continued through 1962 with frequent mentions of the beacon. Sometimes it was inspected daily. The one interesting tidbit I uncovered in my four hours of reading the logs was throughout the 1930s – 1960s, the

Jerry Dowd (left) showing 50,000-watt transmitter to Bob White - photo by Vicky Kaseorg

beacon was always referred to as either the "rotating" or "revolving" beacon. After 1962, the nomenclature changed. There were entries until 1965 about a revolving beacon, but now it included the word "hazard" in some entries. I pointed this out to Jerry.

"This is what I think," I told him, "In the 30s-50s, the engineers all knew it was an airways beacon of the Red 7 airways, and not a hazard beacon. In 1962, the function of the beacon was transferred (we think) to the national bank building, and it was no longer needed for the airways. At that point, its primary function became a hazard beacon."

"That sounds right," said Jerry.

Presumably over the years, Bob White never thought to mention to anyone what he knew was the original function, and no one apparently thought to ask him. Bob and I continued digging through the materials. One of the exciting finds was a hand drawn picture of Tower A, presumably by a Blaw Knox engineer, conceptualizing the first tower. It has to be one of the very few surviving pictures by that famous company of the rare diamond design.

I found the entries describing the rebuild in the 90s. Ted Bryan had kept meticulous records in his neat handwriting of each rebuilt tower section as it was laboriously stacked on the growing tower base. On 11/11/1990, the log entry reported: "repairs completed." On 4/10/1991, the station was fully operational again.

Knowing Ted and his love of the towers as well as his admiration for Tony, I half expected to see an entry lauding the remarkable achievement. But there was nothing like that, just the concise and neat proclamation, "fully operational."

As I sat back from my perusal of that final log entry about the rebuild, Bob exclaimed, "Proof positive!" I hoped he had found something about the beacon, but it was a copy of the original license of the station.

"Look at this," he said. He pointed to the licensing date at the bottom of the document: "satisfactory proof has been furnished that the station was actually operating August 13, 1912. C.H. Euston, Secretary of Commerce."

"What does this prove?" I asked Bob, who was snapping pictures and beaming like a beacon.

"That WBT-AM is the oldest operating radio station in the United States," he said, "Put that in your book."

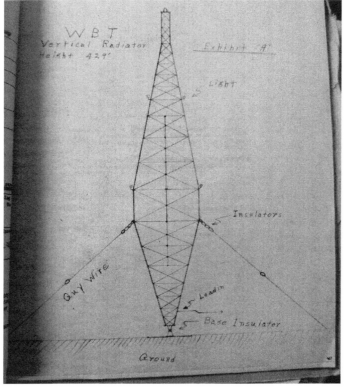

Original Tower A Drawing by Blaw Knox Engineer - WBT-AM Archives

*****

Later, looking at the slides Ted's son had given me, I saw the handsome young Tony, surveying the towers, scurrying over the damaged sections measuring the broken pieces. I saw Ted in the background, a smile on his face, looking on with evident satisfaction. I saw the construction manager's family, the tower riggers, as they tramped about the field and over the tower, welding, cutting, tightening, dangling hundreds of feet in the air. I saw the giant crane lifting away the tattered remains. I saw the pieces neatly laid out on the field, and then the scraps loaded on the huge flatbed truck and carted away. I saw the giant reconstructed sections painted with mitts on the workers' hands, dripping with cherry red and bright white paint. I saw the critical connector piece slowly hoisted through the air. I saw it lowered, closer and closer to the base that had waited for so many months. I saw it settle perfectly into position, with not even a millimeter discrepancy. I saw the gin pole raised, with an American flag fluttering from the top and then each section by section hoisted to the top of the gin pole and lowered atop the growing tower. And then I saw the top piece, capped by the u-bolt and the flashing red beacon, uplifted and placed, and the tower was finished. The last slide was of three diamond shaped towers, lined up like soldiers, brilliantly beautiful against the blue sky.

I could hardly believe there had been a time in my life when I had not noticed them. If I had met Bob the day I started my quest to solve the beacon mystery, I might never have written the book. If it had all been laid out for me beforehand, what would have been the point? What if the blueprints had been available when the towers came crashing down? Would someone as talented and courageous as Tony have been needed?

Imagine if those many years ago when my brother asked me to take photos of archaic towers, I had not bothered? Think of all I would have lost -- all the people I would not have met, all the mystery and wonder I would have missed, all the miracles of discovery I would not have witnessed!

I looked at the three perfect towers and thought to myself, "I love them."

The engineer rebuilt towers without blueprints, only to discover the blueprints had been there all along.

I had solved the mystery of the beacon only to discover the person who knew the solution had been there all along.

We walk by faith, not by sight, but the object of our faith has been there...all along.

*****

Vicky Kaseorg and the Blaw Knox Towers - photo by Bob White

Psalm 61:3 (NIV)
For you have been my refuge, a strong tower against the foe

In Memoriam

Ted Bryan passed away in August 2013. He had had a chance to see the chapters about him, though he died before this book was published. I am indebted to him for his kindness in taking my daughter and myself under wing on that first tour so long ago of the WBT-AM Towers. Little did I know at the time where it would lead.

I picture Ted, alongside many of the WWII veterans I interviewed, in a better place. I suspect that now Ted knows for sure who installed the beacon, and why. One day, in that place of perfect knowledge, I hope to meet him again and let him tell me the whole story.

Acknowledgements

I am indebted to so many wonderful people, including all the characters mentioned in this story. Many generous souls helped with editing and reading the early drafts, giving valuable feedback and encouragement. Many read multiple revisions! I am so grateful to John B. Ceccherelli, Bernice Ceccherelli, Karissa Kaseorg, Amy Fox, and Carol Mayhew who went far above the call of duty with their careful attention to my work and excellent suggestions, as well as specific meticulous editing to multiple versions of this book.

Heart-felt thanks to Brian and Melissa Stewart who spent hours helping me with formatting issues, as well as talking me down when I was ready to throw my computer against the wall.

Special gratitude goes to my experts in their field, who gave so many hours to my persistent questions, and never chastised me for pestering them. Thank you John Eney, Steven Wolff, Jerry Dowd, and Bob White!

Because of these kind and generous people, as well as the heroes of my story, it is a better book, and I am a better person.

Bibliography

1. 26 July 2012. Web. 03 Sept. 2012. <http://www.faa.gov/air_traffic/publications/atpubs/aim/aim0202.html>.

2. Abandoned and Little Known Airfields: NC. 2002. Web. <http://www.airfields-freeman.com/NC/Airfields_NC_Charlotte.htm#delta>.

3. Airmail Division Routes. Web. 3 Sept. 2012. <http://bluegrassairlines.com/bgam/routes.html>.

4. "Battle of the Beams." Wikipedia. Wikimedia Foundation, 09 Mar. 2012. Web. 03 Sept. 2012. <http://en.wikipedia.org/wiki/Battle_of_the_Beams>.

5. Bridgman, Leonard. *Jane's All the World's Aircraft 1942*, Macmillan, 1943. Print

6. Bureau of Air Commerce. 1938, Pg. 140

7. Bureau of Air Commerce. Vol. 9 ,Oct. 15, 1937 No.4 of the Air Commerce Bulletin, Pg. 80.

8. "Carpenter's Airport (Charlotte, North Carolina)(Charlotte, North Carolina)." Carpenter's Airport Charlotte, North Carolina. Web. 03 Sept. 2012. <http://wikimapia.org/12658690/Carpenter-s-Airport>.

9. "Charlotte Aircraft Corporation." Wikipedia. Wikimedia Foundation, 17 Aug. 2012. Web. 27 Aug. 2012. <http://en.wikipedia.org/wiki/Charlotte_Aircraft_Corporation>.

10. Charlotte Sectional Sept. 1943, issued by the Secretary of Commerce, U.S. Coast and Geodetic Survey, Washington D.C.

11. "Code Beacon and Obstruction Lamps for Towers or Bridges." Code Beacon and Obstruction Lamps for

Towers or Bridges. Web. 03 Sept. 2012.
<http://www.budgetlighting.com/store/agora.cgi?page=
code_beacon_obstruction_lamps.html>.
12. "Crystal Radio Page." Crystal Radio Page. Web. 03
Sept.2012.<http://www.hobbytech.com/crystalradio/cry
stalradio.html>.
13. Descriptions of Airports and Landing Fields In The
United States, 1 Jan. 1937. Pg. 140 Published by The
Department of Commerce, Bureau of Air Commerce
Airway Bulletin # 2 (Washington, D.C.) gives the info
about WBT-AM red rotating 24" beacon with red
course lights and 430' antenna 8 miles SSE.
14. Directory of All Radio/FSS Stations. Web. 3 Sept.
2012. < Airmail Division Routes. Web. 3 Sept. 2012.
15. "Eddie Rickenbacker Collection - Auburn
University Special Collections and Archives." Eddie
Rickenbacker Collection - Auburn University Special
Collections and Archives. Auburn University. Web. 03
Sept. 2012. <http://www.lib.auburn.edu/archive/find-
aid/101/eddie.htm>.
16. The Federal Airways System 1970. By The Institute
of Electrical and Electronic Engineers. 1970.
17. Fybush, Scott. "A Selection from a Decade of Visits
to Tower and Studio Sites in the Northeast and
beyond." A Selection from a Decade of Visits to Tower
and Studio Sites in the Northeast and beyond. 5 Dec.
2008. Web. 03 Sept. 2012.
<http://www.fybush.com/sites/2008/site-081205.html>.
18. "General Airway information" Airway Bulletin No.
1 Sept. 1,1931. GPO.
19. Hawkins, Jim "Blaw Knox Diamond Radio
Towers." Blaw Knox Diamond Radio Towers. 1 Mar.

2001. Web. 9 July 2005.
<http://hawkins.pair.com/blaw-knox.html>.
20. "History of Air Depot Detachment, United Aero Services, Delta Air Base, Charlotte, NC". Army Air Force Declassified document. Nov. 1943- April 1944.
21. "Hurricane Hugo." Wikipedia. Wikimedia Foundation, 11 Feb. 2012. Web. 02 Nov. 2012.
<http://en.wikipedia.org/wiki/Hurricane_Hugo>.
22. "Lycoming Engines." Wikipedia. Wikimedia Foundation, 18 Sept. 2012. Web. 18 Sept. 2012.
<http://en.wikipedia.org/wiki/Lycoming_Engines>.
23. Lusch, Thomas. "Using the ADF to Stay Upright." 1990.Web.<http://www.glasair.org/Site/Members/News letter/Issues/38_3_90.pdf>.
24. Jessup, Frederick P. "The Reminiscences of Preston R. Bassett," in the collection of the Columbia Oral History Research Office (54 leaves).1980.
25. "Jim Hawkins' WLW." Transmitter Page. 24 Aug. 1997.Web.03 Sept. 2012.
<http://hawkins.pair.com/wlw.shtml>.
26. "NATE Safety Resources." Â» The National Association of Tower Erectors. 2012. Web. 29 Aug. 2012. <http://natehome.com/safety-education/1893-2/>.
27. "Pilots of America Message Board." Pilots of America Message Board. Nov. 2011. Web. 03 Sept. 2012.
<http://www.pilotsofamerica.com/forum/showthread.php?s=1db4ff1b0629ca9c38679bd557f7d38a>.
28. "Professionalism/Collapse of the TV Antenna in Missouri City, Texas." - Wikibooks, Open Books for an Open World. N.p., n.d. Web. 16 Jan. 2013.

29. "Radio Direction Finder." Wikipedia. Wikimedia Foundation, 28. Aug. 2012. Web. 03 Sept. 2012. <http://en.wikipedia.org/wiki/Radio_direction_finder>.

30."Radio Discussion Board- WBT-AM." RadioDiscussions.com Discussion Boards » Charlotte-Gastonia-Rock Hill » WBT-AM's Signal. Oct. 2006 Web. <http://boards.radioinfo.com/smf/index.php?topic=519 03.20;wap2>.

31. Schamel, John. "Night Navigation Nocturnal Travels." Night Navigation. 31 Jan. 2011. Web. 03 Sept. 2012. <http://www.atchistory.org/History/nightnav.htm>.

32. Smith, Frank K. Legacy of Wings- The Harold E. Pitcairn Story. New York: Jason Aronson, 1981. Print.

33. "Tower-pro : Message: RE: [Tower-pro] Red Light on Roof of WBT-AM TX Building?" Tower-pro : Message: RE: [Tower-pro] Red Light on Roof of WBT-AM TX Building? Web.03Sept.2012.<http://finance.groups.yahoo.com/gr oup/Tower-pro/message/61889>.

34. WBT-AM's Signal. 23 Oct. 2006. Web. <http://boards.radio-info.com/smf/index.php?action=printpage;topic=51903. 0>.

35. Wolff, Steven. "The Federal Airway System- The Early Years." Web. 3 Sept. 2012. <http://www.airwaypioneers.com/Sentinels_of_the_Air ways.pdf>.

36. US Coast and Geodetic Survey, Sept. 9, 1943, Sectional Map of Charlotte area, printed Washington, DC

Other Books by Vicky Kaseorg

I'm Listening with a Broken Ear- 2011
God Drives a Tow Truck- 2011
Tommy- a Story of Ability- 2012
Turning Points-The Life of a Milne Bay WWII Gunner-
2012
The Illustrated 23rd Psalm- 2012
The Good Parent- 2012
The Well-Trained Human- 2012
Saving a Dog- 2014

What the Reviewers Are Saying About Vicky Kaseorg

Listening with a Broken Ear:

*I was pleasantly surprised that the book read well. Vicky is a very good writer.

*This book is simply amazing, one of the best non-fiction books I've read in a very long time.

*This is a wonderful book. The author has a remarkable sense of humor and had me laughing out loud at her remarks

God Drives a Tow Truck:

*The precision, depth, tone and tenor in her writing is exquisite

*I wish I could give this book 6 stars. It is a delight. Inspiring, heart warming mmm mmm good. A must read

*I love this book! It is so awesome and inspiring! These stories touched my core and made me want to deepen my faith more. I hope the author writes another one.

Tommy- A Story of Ability:

*A simple story of acceptance of who (or what) you are, rising above your circumstance to let yourself be happy, and (if you read between the lines) knowing that God simply don't make no junk. Not since Stein's dog Enzo wrote "The Art of Racing in the Rain" has another

doggy author touched the heart strings with their philosophical approach to life.

* quote an old song title, Tommy had the right idea - accentuate the positive and eliminate the negative. And he doesn't seem to mess with Mr. In-Between either. So by now I guess you can tell that I'm not one of your younger readers but that certainly didn't keep me from enjoying this well-written, upbeat little book on a day when I really needed something positive to focus on.

*What a wonderful book! I loved every minute of it. She writes beautifully and anyone that is an animal lover (or even an animal "liker") will love this book. She has a way with words that leave all of us feeling better when we've read the book. From the time this little puppy was sent down the chute to become available for adoption until....oh, never mind, I don't want to give it away.....the story held my interest.

I highly recommend this book - and any other she has written!

Please visit my facebook page and "like" it for regular updates on new books/writing.

https://www.facebook.com/pages/Vicky-Kaseorg-Author/344952178879131

If you enjoyed this book, please go to Amazon, and write a review!

Addendum

ADF
Automatic Direction Finding
By Steven Wolff

I worked on ADF's in the Air Force and used them frequently as a pilot. The common one in the 50's and 60's on military aircraft was the ARN-6. ADF's consist of a receiver, two antennas, a control box and a rotating compass card or fixed compass card and headsets or speakers. Each type of card has a needle that can rotate or point to a station that is tuned in by the pilot or navigator. The receiver is mounted in the plane somewhere and may or may not be accessible to the crew. The control box is accessible to the pilot or navigator. The compass card is displayed at the navigator's position and is usually slaved to one at the pilot's position. The antennas consist of a loop antenna and a sense antenna. This antenna business is VERY IMPORTANT which I'll explain later.

The control box has several functions. One selector knob will select ANT (antenna only) Compass (both antennas) or loop. In the loop function you can turn the loop antenna electrically through 360°. You can also select voice function (AM station) or CW (continuous wave) for code reception. It also has a selector for the reception band of AM broadcast from 200kc to 1750. The 200- 450 band is for low frequency radio range flying. The band from 500? to 1750 is the standard AM (amplitude modulation) radio station. And volume control. All the pilot or navigator does is look at his chart (map) or look for the frequency he wants to use, and tunes it in by identifying the station. The needle will only point to the station if the selector is in the compass position. If the needle points to the nose of the plane, the station is in front, if the needle points to the tail, the station is behind the plane.

Antenna's: The ADF receiver's (same as household radio) have what is called 180° ambiguity. As I said before one antenna is a loop. It looks like a round hoop and is mounted on the top or bottom of the plane. On old planes of the 30's and 40's you can see these. Later they were enclosed in something that looks like a football for aerodynamics. The electrical characteristics of a loop antenna are such that if the hoop(or loop) is at exactly 90° to the received energy from the AM station current flows equally in each side of the loop and cancels out. You would hear this in your headsets as a null or minimum signal. As the loop is turned so that one side is exactly parallel to the received signal you would hear maximum volume. The loop can be turned by: turning the plane for the greatest signal or using the control box.

The problem with the loop antenna only is that there are two positions for a null and a two for a maximum signal. Which means with a loop antenna only, you can't tell if you are going to or flying away from the station.

The sense antenna solves this ambiguity by receiving the tuned station signal from any angle and comparing it electronically with that received by the loop. Sense *antennas are usually a series of wires very small (car aerials are sense antennas) in the canopy of the plane. In the past they were on reel and the antenna had a weight like a fishing weight on the end and it was let out the bottom back of the plane. When you were done, you reeled it back in. They had a shearing mechanism to cut the wire in case it got stuck. They also hung below the plane and would get hung up on trees, etc. Pilots like to let these out when flying over the coast in the fog. They would descend until they could hear loud static in the headsets as the weight struck the water!*

So, the sense antenna solves the ambiguity. Now, to use one ADF in flight. You're out over the ocean and lost. You tune into a station from memory or chart, turn the selector to compass (two antennas) and watch the needle move on the compass card. The head of the needle represents the station and the tail of the needle is the plane. Let's say the needle is dead ahead (lucky). You still don't know where you are except on a line of reciprocal bearing from the station. You draw a line on your map reflecting the needle bearing. You could be ten miles or 1000 miles from the station, so you tune in one more station and watch the needle move when it stops, you note the bearing and draw a line to that station's bearing, and where the two cross is where you are. The more bearings taken, the better.

Now if you just want to home to the station, you just tune it in and keep the needle pointed to the nose of the plane and you do this by turning the plane to keep the needle centered on the nose as you pass over the station, the needle pointer will swing to the rear of the plane(showing that you are now flying away from the station). If you have no wind from either side you will scribe a straight line across the surface of the earth (and pilots are only interested in their track across the ground). If there is a wind, the needle will slowly move to one side and if you do not compensate you will fly to the station in a curve which takes more time and fuel. This is where tracking comes in.

Tracking is flying a straight course across the ground compensating for wind drift. With an ADF, it's done by trial and error. Let's say while flying to a station the needle moves slowly to the right. This means you have wind from the right, so you look at the tail of the needle and see that is 20° to the left (needle on the nose is 20° to the right). To get back on course you double your correction (20+20) 40° to the right and see what happens. It may be too much or not enough. You will eventually find a heading that will keep the needle on the bearing to the station and you will track straight across the ground.

Here's where the stupids get in trouble. As a crosscheck to tell if you're flying to the station or away from it, is the volume control. As the plane gets closer to the station the volume will get louder and of course less as you fly away, so you don't want to constantly fiddle with the volume control.

The ADF's are beset by all kinds of reception errors, lightning, sky waves, man-made static, precipitation static (rain). All this causes the compass needle to move around erratically.

Sky waves are caused at night when the ionosphere cools and cause the AM stations transmissions to bounce off (the ionosphere) and come down in unlikely places and mileages. That's way AM stations cut the power down at sunset. In the day time power is increased but the ionosphere is active with holes and the strong signals go out in to space.

There is good evidence that our friend Amelia Earhart left her trailing antenna in Papua New Guinea. In one of her conversations, she told the Itasca (the ship she was supposed to home in on) that she was receiving a minimum, which meant she was working the radio and using the loop, but couldn't tell if she was flying towards or away from the Itasca. She had other problems with communications in selecting the frequency on the HF radio she was using. She was using the wrong frequency for the time of day. HF (high frequency) radios have crazy characteristics at sunrise and sunset (ionosphere again). And as she was arriving near sunrise or early morning her reception was not all that good. She was told this, by the way, in her pre flight preparations by the Navy. (What do they know!) Nearly all of the ocean flyers at that time period said they would rather have a good radio operator than navigator. I always used to remember to hunt for the HF frequencies: the higher the sun, the higher the frequency. But sometimes that doesn't even work so you try them all. I made lots of ocean crossings in three and four engine jets and never considered any of them routine."

VICKY KASEORG

If you liked this book, please write a review at amazon.com or any site where you purchased this book online. Thank you!

Hoisting the flag to the top of the tower - courtesy Ted Bryan estate